Eugene Kinckle Jones

EUGENE KINCKLE JONES

*The National Urban League
and Black Social Work, 1910–1940*

Felix L. Armfield

University of Illinois Press
Urbana, Chicago, and Springfield

Library of Congress Cataloging-in-Publication Data
Armfield, Felix L. (Felix Lionel)
Eugene Kinckle Jones : the National Urban League
and Black social work, 1910–40 / Felix L. Armfield.
p.   cm.
Includes bibliographical references and index.
ISBN 978-0-252-03658-3 (cloth)
1. Jones, Eugene Kinckle, 1885–1954.
2. African American social reformers—Biography.
3. National Urban League—History—20th century.
I. Title.
HN64.A76   2011
303.48'4092—dc23 [B]   2011029266

For black social workers,
past, present, and future.

Contents

Illustrations follow page 22

Acknowledgments

This work would not have been possible had my mentor Darlene Clark Hine not insisted that I look at the papers of the National Urban League. I approached this project with some reluctance and did not understand all that Professor Hine was expecting of it. I suppose she forgave my graduate-student innocence. Words could never thank her enough for the time and energy she has devoted to this project. Her stellar mentoring continues to inspire a new generation of historians.

In addition to Professor Hine, several other individuals' scholarship and teaching assisted this project and me as a graduate student. Dr. Fred Honhart read and commented on every page of my dissertation with unwavering attention; I thank him for his enormous support. Professors Harry Reed and David Robinson were crucial to my early development in graduate studies. Their seminars challenged me to think in meaningful and helpful ways. Professor Richard Thomas's teachings on race relations and the black urban condition introduced me to new ways of organizing the black community. Professor Thomas, thanks for all the "self-help." In addition to my Michigan State University mentors, a number of individuals have supported me and my work. Ms. Linda Werbish was always available to assist me and saw to it that my deadlines and timetables were appropriately met. I owe Professor Rosalyn Terborg-Penn of Morgan State University for all her continued support. Dr. Terborg-Penn first introduced me to the Jones family; I could not have completed this project without her. In addition, thanks to all of my professors at North Carolina Central University for demanding nothing less than my best.

I would be remiss if I did not thank my colleagues at Western Illinois University for all their support and encouragement from every entity of the institution. My friends and colleagues in the Department of History and African American Studies were supportive of this project from the dissertation phase onward. However, the historian Larry Balsamo read every page of the dissertation in rough draft, and his comments challenged me to think and write with greater clarity. His dedication will long be remembered. The historian Tom Watkins gave me my first lessons on Cornell University, his alma mater. Watkins shared with me his personal collection of materials on Cornell, and I truly thank him and his wife, Sharon Watkins, for sharing their library with me. In addition, I wish to thank my new family of colleagues at Buffalo State College for helping to create a conducive environment for my research.

The library staff at Western Illinois University deserves more thanks than I could ever offer here for their unceasing assistance. The reference department proved to be my greatest asset. John Steinman and Kathy Dahl were always available to answer my questions, and Kathy found resources that only an excellent reference librarian could have located. No query or request was too monumental for her. The staff of the Social Welfare History Archives assisted my research with enthusiasm. The people at the Virginia State Archives were very helpful, providing me with all requested materials in a timely manner. Cornell University Archives staff also provided helpful information by revealing Eugene Kinckle Jones's student records. Ms. Beth Howse, the Special Collection Librarian at Fisk University Archives, was helpful during my search. In addition, she is the granddaughter of one of the founding members of the original Fisk Jubilee Singers.

Since graduate school, this work on Eugene Kinckle Jones has taken on new life. I have had far more conversations than I care to recall. I am grateful to many friends, colleagues, mentors, and students who had no choice but to listen. There have been many late-night talks while attending the annual meetings of the Association for the Study of African American Life and History and the Organization of American Historians. Thanks to a host of historians and colleagues for engaging me: Richard Pierce, Priscilla Dowden-White, Elsa Barkley Brown, Stephanie Shaw, Thavolia Glymph, Freddie Parker, Leslie Brown, Annie Valk, Shirley Portwood, Stefan Bradley, Derrick Aldridge, Chana Kai Lee, Lillian Williams, Betty Gardner, June O. Patton, Wanda Hendricks, Dana Ramey-Berry, Michelle Mitchell, Carlton Wilson, Lydia Lindsey, Ula Taylor, Paul Ortiz, Nikki Taylor, Scott Brown, Allison Dorsey, Vincent P. Franklin, and Linda Causey. A thoughtful thanks belongs to my social-work-scholar sisters, Drs. Iris Carlton-LaNey and N. Yolanda Burwell. They helped me to begin thinking like social workers. A very special thanks goes to the historian Genna Rae McNeil for taking time out from her own work to read my manuscript in its entirety over 2003–4. Professor McNeil asked hard questions and encouraged me to improve my work in areas I might have otherwise overlooked; she is a first-rate biographer and a gracious mentor. In addition, my support network at Buffalo State College continues to be vital. To my newfound friends and extended family in the city of Buffalo, I am eternally grateful. Moreover, Professor Robert Harris of Cornell University, the national historian of Alpha Phi Alpha fraternity, gave me the most rewarding review of my work to date. His critique was thorough and saved me major mistakes in the final draft. His devotion to this project is unparalleled; Professor Harris helped to make this a worthwhile work.

I could not have made it through the graduate program at Michigan State University had it not been for the support of some friends in particular. To Jacqueline McLeod, thanks for being the dearest friend I could have ever hoped for. Randall Jelks, thanks for being my soul brother. Quince and Kelly Brinkley helped me to keep it all real, despite what I may have been up against. My best friend on the planet, Diane "Cookie" Pippins, has been my reality check longer than I care to recall these days. Last but certainly not least, Judge Taylor, Greg Osborn, Darryl Daniels, Brent Price, Gerald Todd, and Ray Howell: thanks for teaching me how to exhale.

I am grateful for the time that Betty Jones Dowling, Eugene Kinckle Jones's granddaughter, allowed me to spend with her as she made all the family photos available within this publication.

I'm glad I know the meaning of family. My family continues to be a constant force in my life. I am truly blessed to have my paternal grandmother, Christine Jenkins Armfield, who always reminded me "to whom I belonged." I thank my sister, Kimberly Armfield, for all her financial and emotional support over the years. My folks, Jasper and the late Alice Armfield: thank you for all the support over the years. I thank my brother, Jeff Armfield, and his family for always cheering me on. And in recent times I have realized that life is tenuous at best. Hopefully this helps to begin to repay all of you in some small way. I can honestly say to you all: Your helpings of "soul food" have been sufficient.

Introduction

This book examines the life and work of Eugene Kinckle Jones (1885–1954), along with the rise of professional black social workers within the larger context of social work and its professionalization. In 1971, Guichard Parris and Lester Brooks published the first major history of the National Urban League (NUL), *Blacks in the City: A History of the National Urban League*. Parris and Brooks put forth this much-needed history during the black-power movement in America. Several factors prompted a need for this history. There was, at the time, no history of the Urban League, and Parris and Brooks wanted to "help to counter the tendency in some quarters to misconstrue the Urban League's efforts and denigrate or ignore its accomplishments."[1] Jones's work and the experiences of black social workers were not their primary focus. Nancy Weiss published *The National Urban League, 1910–1940*, in 1974; while she chronicles the history of the NUL from its beginnings, her work pays little attention to the details of Jones's life and the opportunities the league offered black social workers, in part, perhaps, because Jones's papers were not yet accessible to scholars. Jesse Thomas Moore Jr. published *A Search for Equality: The National Urban League, 1910–1961*, in 1981, in which he argues that the NUL had grown from a social-reform movement into a national institution of strictly racial and social concerns by 1961. Here again, Jones and black social workers receive little attention. Edyth I. Ross published a quick reference source in 1978, *Black Heritage in Social Welfare, 1860–1930*, but her work lacks historical perspective and content. None of these histories identifies Jones as the central figure in the NUL or underscores his role in the American social-work movement. This study will examine the early-twentieth-century black social-work movement, placing particular emphasis on Jones's life and work with the National Urban League. This is not a history of the NUL as an organization; it is a study of one of its most significant leaders: Eugene Kinckle Jones.

Through the National Urban League, along with the work of professionally trained black social workers, Jones fought against racial discrimination against African American migrants to northern cities. This study will increase our knowledge of the "urban black experience" and how African Americans helped to shape that experience in ways that allowed them to survive. The main focus of this study, however, is on Jones and his role in the professionalization of black social work. It will be revealed that his leadership of the National Urban League and his involvement with black and white social reformers early in the twentieth century was instrumental in the development of black social work.

Though the focus of this study is on Eugene Kinckle Jones, it would be difficult to tell his story without revealing some of the history of the NUL. Jones was the leader of this major black protest organization in the first half of the twentieth century, and he helped to define and characterize this noted American institution. In addition to his work as the leader of the NUL, Jones played a major role in the development of professional social work. Jones's tenure coincided with the Great Migration of southern African Americans to northern cities. As a result of this urbanization process, the urgency for black social workers was great. In essence, the fate of these professionals was inextricably connected to the survival of black urban migrant communities.

This study will reveal the numerous fronts on which Jones and his contemporaries fought to make professional black social work a reality. Jones solicited funds, delivered speeches, wrote articles, served in the federal government, established NUL branches all over the country, and became the first noted statesman of the league. By 1940, upon his retirement, social work for African Americans had spread throughout the nation in both rural and urban areas. This study will establish Jones as a major contributor to that process and a leading African American intellect of the early twentieth century.

Eugene Kinckle Jones was born in 1885. Oddly enough, he grew up in an integrated environment in Richmond, Virginia. Jim Crow segregation by the late nineteenth century was entrenched throughout the South and was quickly becoming customary throughout the entire United States. Jones and his family resided in an all-black neighborhood in Richmond, referred to as the "black ward" of Jackson. Both of Jones's parents were well educated and taught in black institutions of higher education. His father, Joseph Endom Jones, taught theology at Virginia Union College; he was the first African American faculty member hired at the college, which was founded for African American students in 1867. Jones's mother, Rosa Kinckle Jones, was a music teacher at the nearby Hartshorn Memorial College for black women. His parents' careers afforded young Jones rare opportunities. As a youth, he witnessed his parents interacting on an equal basis with white intellectuals, and this left an impression on him. Few black youngsters could recall having experiences of this kind at the turn of the twentieth century. In 1905, Jones received his bachelor's degree from Virginia Union College for Negroes. He was nurtured within an environment that insisted on great achievements.

Upon the completion of his studies at Virginia Union, Jones enrolled at Cornell University in Ithaca, New York, to pursue a master's degree. He began to work toward a degree in mathematics and engineering, but after one year he changed his major. Jones completed his studies at Cornell in the spring of 1908 with a master's degree in economics and social science. With impressive credentials in hand, Jones confronted the color line. He could only secure employment as a schoolteacher in private and public schools for blacks in Louisville, Kentucky, where he encountered the man who would change his life. In 1911, Jones met with the prominent black sociologist Dr. George Edmund Haynes, who proposed that he come to New York and work for the newly formed League on Urban Conditions among Negroes.

The historian Ralph E. Luker points out that the social gospel was in vogue during Jones's formative years. In *The Social Gospel in Black and White: American Racial Reform, 1885–1912* (1991), Luker makes a compelling case for the roles played by African Americans in the Reform Era. Jones was born in 1885, and by 1912 he had completed his formal education. In addition to the social gospel of racial reform, Jones and his peers represented the first generation of African Americans that had no experience with the infamous "peculiar institution," slavery. Though they were the first to confront the reality of Jim Crow and the *Plessy v. Ferguson* ruling of "separate but equal," the first generation of free-born African Americans was emboldened to buy into the social-gospel method of reform. Within the era of Jim Crow segregation, the social gospel flourished. The historian Earl E. Thorpe argued that the Progressive Era (1901–17) in "Black America produced its own very important Muckrakers and Progressive Movement" and that Jones belonged to this group of reform- and progressive-minded individuals in the late nineteenth and early twentieth centuries.[2]

Jones arrived in New York in 1911 to accept the position of field secretary of the League on Urban Conditions among Negroes, now renamed the National Urban League. His job would soon engage his energies on two different fronts: he became an active advocate for black migrants, and he worked to legitimize the black social worker's professional authority. Jones's first major task involved assessing and reporting on the conditions of black life in the inner city of New York. He assumed the responsibility for helping migrants become acculturated to their new urban environments. Often he met new arrivals at the train depot and assisted them in finding housing and employment. Jones met with personnel in industries and firms to discuss and arrange for expanded employment opportunities, as many had quotas for black hiring. Black migrants were frequently used as strikebreakers, which fueled the flames of hostility among white workers.

The duties of black social workers and the aims of the NUL included evaluating and reviewing settlement houses, in addition to other specific concerns of migrating blacks. Black social workers intervened with employment bureaus on behalf of juveniles and adults; they also helped negotiate contracts for black men. They placed workers in industrial plants and generally tried to raise the efficiency of African American laborers. Black social workers also paid attention to health-care concerns and provided home-economic guidance to families in need of help with budgets and preparing nutritious food.

In 1916, Jones was appointed executive secretary of the NUL. Over the next four years, the northward migration of black men and women increased greatly. As director of the NUL, Jones was compelled to seek the assistance of social workers. Jones and other black social workers tried to convince white social workers of the need to address the race question. Jones tried to unify the mission of black and white social workers as early as 1921. He devised a plan of action for the black social-work movement based upon the practice of racial integration. The plan made many white social workers uncomfortable; they sought to separate their mission from that of black social workers for fear that they would not be recognized as professionals by the larger society. The American Association of Social Workers (AASW) in the early twentieth century sought to have social work recognized as a profession equal to that of law and medicine. The AASW was not interested in the racial integration of the profession, so Jones and other prominent black social workers participated in the umbrella organization for all social work, National Conference of Social Work (NCSW).

Chapter 1 of this book provides a contextualized background for the life of Eugene Kinckle Jones. Although circumscribed by the limits of Jim Crow, Jones made key decisions that affected his entire life. This chapter will detail his life from its beginnings in Richmond, as he matriculated through Virginia Union College for Negroes and later Cornell University. Both institutions helped to shape his life and opinions. Eventually, his educational experience would propel him before the nation as a leader of social work and an advocate for institutional cooperation among the races. Chapter 2 traces the history of the National Urban League with a specific focus on Jones's leadership. This chapter covers the decade of the 1920s and the many issues that Jones and his contemporaries confronted. Chapter 3 examines the NUL as Jones penetrated the executive ranks of the NCSW. In this capacity, he gained valuable resources for the further training of black social workers, as well as financial and educational support for his cause. The NCSW provided a national and integrated audience for addressing the social woes of black America. Jones's involvement with the federal government is the core of chapter 4. He was an integral member of Franklin D. Roosevelt's Black Cabinet during the New Deal. This chapter examines how black social workers responded to "relief" efforts and the ways they facilitated institution building and community development during the 1930s. Chapter 5 discusses Jones's resignation from the position of executive secretary of the Urban League in 1940 and the assumption of the title of general secretary until 1950. Following the Great Depression, the complexity of state and federal intervention drastically changed social-work programs. Chapter 5 concludes with an overview of Jones's work and life from 1940 until his retirement in 1950.

This study of Jones, the NUL, and the American social-work movement will increase our understanding of the processes of migration and of migrants becoming black urbanites. I will not discuss the nature of social work as labor. Rather, I will illustrate how social work as a profession engaged black Americans and how it was administered during its infancy. Moreover, I will explore the "causes" rather than the "function" of social welfare as it developed for black people. The movement to increase the number of professionally trained black social workers gained momentum from the large numbers of blacks who migrated north during the First World War. As immigration sanctions became inevitable by 1914, the need for black southern labor grew urgent. Many blacks took this opportunity to free themselves and their children of the ravages of southern oppression. Many saw the North as the Promised Land. Little did they know that the North held its own forms of oppression.

Scholars such as Elisabeth Lasch-Quinn and Michael B. Katz reveal that Jim Crow proscriptions abounded in the Promised Land. In *Black Neighbors: Race and the Limits of Reform in the American Settlement House Movement, 1890–1945* (1993), Lasch-Quinn argues that the American social-reform movement did not reach out to southern black migrants. Katz's book, *In the Shadow of the Poorhouse: A Social History of Welfare in America* (1986), makes clear that white settlement-house reformers did not welcome migrating blacks. The need for and the rise of professional black social workers developed as a consequence of this racial divide within the social-work movement.

1. From Richmond to Ithaca

May the true spirit of fraternity rule our hearts,
guide our thoughts, and control our lives, so that
we may become, through thee, servants of all.
—Alpha Phi Alpha, Fraternity Prayer

Eugene Kinckle Jones was born on July 30, 1885, to Joseph Endom Jones (1850–1922) and Rosa Daniel Kinckle Jones (1857–1931) of Richmond, Virginia. His parents were natives of Lynchburg, Virginia. Joseph Jones was born a slave in 1850.[1] The Jones family traces its lineage to Sicily Jones, the slave of Maurice Langhorne. The Langhornes were longtime Virginia aristocrats.[2] An invalid Confederate soldier taught Joseph Endom Jones to read and write during the Civil War.

Joseph Jones left Lynchburg for Richmond after the war, where he enrolled in Virginia Union University (formerly the Richmond Institute, sometimes referred to as Richmond Theological Seminary). The site had served as Lumpkin's jail, where Union prisoners were incarcerated; ironically, it was originally the location of Robert Lumpkin's slaveholding pens. The structure was "a two-story brick house with barred windows, located in the heart of Richmond's famous slave market"—considered by local blacks as "the Devil's Half Acre."[3] Many black men and women saw Richmond as a symbol of the North's victory. At the end of March 1865, as the northern armies were surging toward Richmond and Petersburg, the final crumbling strongholds of southern resistance, black Union troops were viewed prominently in the moving lines of men.[4]

Joseph Jones remained in Richmond until 1869, when a Norwich, Connecticut, bookbinder who was touring the South encouraged and supported his educational aspirations. He was sent by the bookbinder to Hamilton, New York, to be enrolled at Hamilton Academy. By 1876, Joseph Jones had completed studies in theology at Colgate University (formerly Hamilton Academy) with the help of northern white supporters. Joseph Jones returned to Richmond, the former capitol of the Confederacy, prepared to assist in the enormous work of educating the recently freed black population, conducted by liberal whites and progressive blacks.[5] Second to only Washington, D.C., Richmond served as a hub of educational activity through the Freedman's Bureau and the American Baptist Home Mission Society.[6] Unfortunately for Joseph Jones, he returned to Richmond at a time of unstable race relations. By 1876, white southerners were claiming redemption over congressional Reconstruction, and African Americans were reduced to second-class citizenship. Blacks in Richmond endured the same fate.

Rosa Daniel Kinckle Jones was born of free lineage in Lynchburg. Rosa's father, John Kinckle, had purchased his freedom, but her mother, Rachel Smith Kinckle, was born to a slave mother and her mother's white master. The master willed at his death that young Rachel be set free when she found a free African American man to marry. He also stipulated that she be given five hundred dollars. John Kinckle seemed a likely suitor. Though a former slave, he experienced an interesting career in the city of Lynchburg. Through "sacrifices, hard work, and self-confidence he gained the monopoly of the express business in his home city."[7] John Kinckle was a porter and baggage handler at the railroad depot in Lynchburg.[8] The city offered more opportunity for personal and material success than southern locales with a smaller black population. "Between 1860 and 1870, census statistics confirmed what the white South had already strongly suspected—a striking increase in the black urban population. . . . Three of Virginia's principal cities—Richmond, Norfolk, and Lynchburg—now had nearly as many blacks as whites," which encouraged many blacks to take their chances at economic success there.[9] Richmond was the likely place of migration for most blacks leaving Lynchburg. Lynchburg was linked to Richmond through the James River and Kanawha Canal (see map 1). By 1860, the railroad had become the most sophisticated means of travel between the two cities.[10] The historian Peter Rachleff concludes, "There were many reasons for coming to the capital. Some [blacks] saw immigration as a celebration of freedom. Black men with skills or particular aspirations might pick Richmond as the site of greater opportunity than existed in the rural areas and small towns."[11] The Kinckle and Jones families' experiences paralleled that described by Robert Francis Engs in *Freedom's First Generation: Black Hampton, Virginia, 1861–1890*. Engs states: "Even in political and economic defeat, black Hampton's first free generation could look with pride at its major achievement: its children. They were well educated, ambitious, sophisticated in business, in education, and in the ways of the world, white as well as black, Northern as well as Southern. They and their descendants

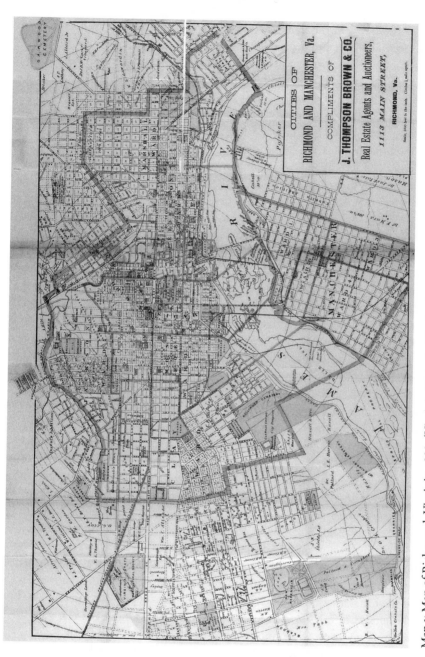

Map 1: Map of Richmond, Virginia, 1888. (Virginia Historical Society)

would continue to play a major role in American black life long after accommodation had been repudiated."[12]

Though neither family was from Hampton, John Kinckle and Sicily Jones were in a position to look to their offspring with much pride. They would represent the best of "freedom's first generation" in Richmond. The historian Vincent Harding puts it best: "[T]he children of bondage were crossing over, bearing visions of a new land, challenging white America to a new life."[13]

The Jones family was unique in the city of Richmond in the late nineteenth century, as the young married couple were both college educated. Joseph and Rosa Jones returned to Richmond by the early 1880s to begin their new lives in a city that had witnessed greater devastation than most southern cities during the latter days of the Civil War. One contemporary recalled, "[T]he future seemed bleak indeed for devastated, bankrupt Richmond, its people hungry and disconsolate, its soldiers returning penniless from the front, and many of its finest young men killed, or maimed for life." A great portion of Richmond's destruction was done by retreating southern troops: "[I]n April 1865 [they] set fire to supplies, arsenals, and bridges," causing more than eight million dollars in damages.[14] The city struggled to mend itself in the aftermath of the war.

It is likely that the parents of Eugene Kinckle Jones knew of each other in their formative years in Lynchburg. Joseph Jones and Rosa Kinckle were married in 1882 in Richmond. Following their marriage vows, the two honeymooned in Norwich, Connecticut. The local papers made mention of a "Negro man and his bride who was the daughter of this former slave, John Kinckle."[15]

The Joneses in Richmond were at the center of the emerging "black elite" or black middle class. One study concludes that E. K. Jones "was born into the black bourgeoisie."[16] At the time of the collapse of Reconstruction in 1877, two aristocracies were evolving in black America: the aristocracy of culture and the aristocracy of wealth. Several factors determined whether one belonged to the black elite, including but not limited to "official station, position in the church, possession of money or real estate, former ownership, and city birth." One other leading concern was that "the color factor was also important in the stratification process." Accordingly, the Joneses and the Kinckles were initiated into the "black aristocracy" by the 1880s and were quite comfortable in its circles. The luxury of traveling to Norwich to honeymoon was growing among this burgeoning black middle class.[17]

Joseph and Rosa Jones, both having attained their college education in the North during Reconstruction, returned to Richmond prepared to help uplift the black populace. The Joneses belonged to the group of African Americans that the historian Kevin Gaines refers to as "race men and women":

they were altruistic in their approach to addressing the problems that beset black America following Reconstruction.[18] They were also strong advocates of group solidarity as a means of racial uplift. In 1876, Joseph Jones was commissioned by the American Baptist Home Mission Society to join the faculty of Richmond Theological Seminary at Virginia Union University, an all-black college, although most of its faculty at the time were white. He was one of the first instructors to aid with the further development of Virginia Union University.

He was eventually promoted to chair of Homiletics and Greek Studies and served the institution until his death in 1922. One contemporary recorded, "Professor Jones is an efficient teacher, a popular and instructive preacher, and a forcible writer."[19] Virginia Union University's majority-white faculty strongly rejected "an emphasis on industrial skills and consciously provided an education for the Talented Tenth." The school was strictly opposed to Booker T. Washington's ideas of racial accomodationism and advocated more liberal attitudes.[20] Though Washington's Tuskegee Institute–model of industrial education was in vogue by the late nineteenth century, it was not the standard for all black colleges. Virginia Union held to its ideals of a liberal-arts educational program. Joseph Jones supported these ideas and transmitted them to his son, Eugene Kinckle Jones. Whether Jones was more aligned with Washington or DuBois would be tested throughout his stint with the NUL. He appears to have been more Washingtonian when it came to the NUL as an institution and its operational procedures. However, in his personal life and professional contacts, he strictly adhered to DuBois's talented-tenth theory.

Rosa Daniel Kinckle graduated from Howard University in 1880, a time when many were still questioning whether women should be educated, and if so to what extent. Rosa Kinckle was one of the first ten women to graduate from Howard's Normal Department.[21] She would receive further training at the New England Conservatory of Music before returning south to Richmond as the wife of Rev. Dr. Joseph E. Jones.[22]

On July 30, 1885, the Joneses gave birth to their first and only child, Eugene Kinckle Jones. Rosa joined the faculty of Hartshorn Memorial College in 1888 as a teacher of music. Hartshorn was established in 1883 for the education of African American girls, and it was named in honor of its donor, Joseph C. Hartshorn of Rhode Island.[23] According to an article in *The Messenger,* the school was always associated with the "choicest women workers." "Its educational standards are high, but most important of all it places special emphasis upon the development of the moral and religious life. Its spirit and life are pre-eminently Christian."[24] Rosa Kinckle Jones belonged to this elite group of Christian women. She served as head of the music department at Hartshorn for forty years.[25] Hartshorn eventually merged with Virginia Union University in 1932, one year after Rosa Jones's death. She worked at the school during a period when it struggled to maintain a separate institutional identity from that of Virginia Union University. Hartshorn's trustees wanted it to remain an institution for African American girls.

Rosa Jones distinguished herself at Hartshorn and within the city of Richmond as a pianist.[26] The historian Rayford Logan stated, "A few, like Rosa D. Kinckle (Mrs. Joseph E. Jones), . . . not only taught but were wives of men who served well their communities and the Nation and were mothers of children who attended excellent schools."[27] The newlyweds settled at 520 St. James Street in Richmond, determined to build a life for themselves and their infant son despite the collapse of Reconstruction and deteriorating race relations.[28] The Jones family home was in the environs of some of Richmond's most prominent black families. Richmond's modest black upper class could boast that "there were similar antebellum concentrations of homeowning free Negroes on Duval, on the 500 block of West Baker . . . St. James, St. Peter, and St. Paul Streets."[29]

During Reconstruction, blacks in Richmond experienced a peculiar level of participation in the city's government and municipalities. The historian Howard Rabinowitz claims that Richmond's blacks were "more fortunate" than those in other southern urban centers during Reconstruction. In 1870, Virginia received its first black justice of the peace in Henrico County, which included Richmond.[30] In 1879, Virginia's former politicians—who were supposedly its "best people"—were removed from both houses of the legislature. By the 1870s, a new group of white leaders who did not belong to Virginia's aristocratic class took office. Many of them were "opportunists and some were even erratic visionaries given to supporting any minority cause."[31] The historian Michael B. Chesson discovered that, ironically, black participation in city government did not begin until after Reconstruction in Richmond, between 1871 and 1896. This can be attributed to the fact that most of Richmond's black populace resided in the all-black Jackson Ward. By the 1890s, Richmond had begun to take steps to rezone the city's traditional voting districts, breaking up Jackson Ward. Some would argue that by the mid-1870s, Virginia was one of the southern states that "had already reverted to Democratic rule."[32] Richmond politics were different than statewide politics as a result of the larger black population.

Between 1871 and 1898, thirty-three blacks held positions on Richmond's city council.[33] Though Reconstruction had ended throughout the South by 1877, blacks in Richmond expressed meaningful hope through participation in the city's new government. Chesson further concludes that political activities historians have usually associated with Reconstruction continued well into the 1890s in Richmond. From 1871 to 1898, blacks in Richmond were visible in "officeholding, widespread voting, alliances with white Republicans of various factions, intense competition for office . . . and variously success-ful Republican appeals to Congress and the federal courts for relief from Bourbon oppression."[34]

In the 1870s, the Richmond city council began efforts to destroy any co-operative race relations in the city, which aided in the further collapse of Re-construction. "Richmond officials sought to confine Negro voters to Jackson Ward in an effort to restrict their political power."[35] By the 1880s, race relations in Richmond, as in much of the South, had significantly deteriorated.[36] Most black citizens were denied city jobs either because of their race or because they were Republicans. The city council created the majority-black ward of Jackson to assure Democratic dominance. Jackson Ward represented the first gerrymandering efforts in Richmond, which allowed for the other five wards to be overwhelmingly Democratic. This contributed to ending radi-cal Reconstruction in Richmond. All of the thirty-three black councilmen represented Jackson Ward. In 1890, 79 percent of the population in Jackson Ward was black. Though 30 percent of the black population lived throughout the white wards, Jackson was commonly referred to as the Black Belt.[37] The Joneses settled in Jackson Ward, "the most famous concentration of blacks."[38] (See map 1.)

Black political power in Richmond was heavily concentrated in Jackson Ward,[39] which was bounded on the west and north by Bacon Quarter Branch, on the east by Shockoe Creek, and to the south by Leigh Street. By 1890, Jackson's black population was 13,530 of Richmond's total black population of 32,330.[40] The Joneses' middle-class status enabled young Eugene Kinckle Jones to see and reach beyond Jackson Ward, where he was born in 1885. This represents the paradoxical nature of freedom's first generation in Richmond.

By the 1890s, cooperative race relations had deteriorated rapidly in the old Confederate capitol. In 1890, a major lack of respect was dealt to the black community of Richmond: city leaders extended an expansion project that "tore up Richmond's historic black cemetery, in which many of the city's most famous slaves and free Negroes had been buried." As a further insult, the relocation of the remains was not revealed.

Three years later, Richmond experienced its first serious financial panic since the war; much suffering, unemployment, and bankruptcy ensued in this panic of the 1890s. Race relations were sorely wounded again by the unveiling of the statue of Robert E. Lee in 1890. While the event attracted a record-setting turnout of Civil War personalities, it was not well received in the black community. The white South had looked forward to the "equestrian statue" for quite some time.[41]

This occasion did not stop the leading black newspaper, the *Richmond Planet*, from attacking Robert E. Lee and all the Confederates.[42] The *Planet* was owned and edited by the black councilman John Mitchell Jr., a "mulatto" who also served on the Richmond city council from 1888 to 1896. Mitchell had adamantly opposed the council's ten-thousand-dollar appropriation for the statue. The day that the unveiling ceremony took place, he objected to it publicly in the *Planet*. He wrote, "The men who talk most about the valor of Lee and the blood of the brave Confederate dead are those who never smelt powder" and further lamented that "most of them were at a table, either on top or under it, when the war was going on." Mitchell openly proclaimed that the event would cement a "legacy of treason and blood." He exhibited enormous courage at a time when lynchings of black men and women in the South were on the increase.[43] Mitchell "was the kind of black leader that white Richmonders hated and feared. Mitchell had had the audacity to ridicule the Confederacy and to campaign openly against the brutal and increasingly frequent practice of lynching."[44] He was not alone in his opposition to the Confederate monument. The *Philadelphia North American* compared Lee to Benedict Arnold; and the *New York Mail and Express* proposed that Congress stop the continued erection of monuments to Confederate heroes as well as the continuing use of the Confederate flag.[45]

Mary White Ovington interviewed Eugene Kinckle Jones for a 1927 publication entitled *Portraits in Color*. When asked what was there to say about himself, he stated, "There's nothing much to say about me." He further noted that he had no "Up from Slavery" story. His father owned the house in which he was born, and he attended some of the finest schools that Richmond had to offer. As a youngster, Jones attended schools that were aided by white northern supporters. He witnessed white and black teachers commingling at Hartshorn and Virginia Union. He also admitted that his parents were in privileged positions compared to most blacks in Richmond and the South generally. Ovington recalled from a photograph that his mother was an "exquisite lady in her black satin with a bit of fine lace at the throat." Perhaps Ovington viewed the photograph in relation to the Joneses' middle-class status. Joseph Jones eventually chaired the Department of Theology at the Richmond Theological Seminary, which became Virginia Union University in 1896.[46]

In 1897, Joseph E. Jones received an invitation to join the American Negro Academy, the first major black American learned society in the United States, which was founded that same year. Its prominent founding members included Alexander Crummell, W. E. B. DuBois, John W. Cromwell, and Kelly Miller. "They tended to be well educated, with a strong sense of race identity, active and effective leaders, and highly respectable."[47] According to its constitution, the American Negro Academy was "an organization of authors, scholars, artists, and those distinguished in other walks of life, men of African descent, for the promotion of Letters, Science, and Art."[48] Joseph Jones never responded to this new black intellectual organization's call. The historian Alfred A. Moss Jr. has declared that all the individuals who were invited to join were stellar in character. The Joneses were pillars of prosperity and hope for many in the black community of Richmond; they represented the advancement that had come to some blacks during Reconstruction.

In spite of mounting adversity, much activity in Richmond during the late 1880s and 1890s was initiated by African American race leaders. Eugene Kinckle Jones recalled in an interview with Gunnar Myrdal in 1940: "In Richmond there was great activity among certain Negro leaders to develop race pride, business ventures, political influence. John Mitchell, the editor of the *Richmond Planet*; D. Webster Davis, the poet and lecturer; W. W. Brown, the founder and president of the Grand United Order of True Reformers; Maggie L. Walker, the first woman president of a bank in the United States and the leader of the St. Luke's Penny Savings Bank—these and many others were active during those days and aroused all Negro young people in Richmond to a high degree of racial consciousness and confidence."[49]

The St. Luke's Penny Savings Bank was created in 1887 by the United Order of True Reformers, a black civic organization that was founded in the late 1870s and "flourished into the twentieth century." The bank represented a major achievement for blacks as an example of an institution that was independently organized, supported, and controlled by black people. The United Order of True Reformers was a visible and active organization during the late nineteenth and early twentieth centuries. The organization provided the black community of Richmond with grocery stores, clothing stores, a hundred-room hotel, a home for the aged, a real-estate firm, a loan association, and an organizational newspaper, *The Reformer*.[50] The historian August Meier found that the social climate of the era favored "group separatism": "It was in the church and fraternity that Negroes found unhampered opportunity for social life and for the exercise of leadership."[51] Richmond's black community appears to have seized the opportunities that grew out of the social realities of Jim Crow.

It is particularly interesting to focus on Richmond. The historian Elsa Barkley Brown argues that "as the former capital of the Confederacy, Richmond is an important place to look at the transition from slavery to freedom."[52]

Richmond's black populace spanned the entire spectrum during this period of political, social, and economic uncertainty. The irony of all of this is that Richmond was one of the first urban centers in the country to allow for black membership in the Knights of Labor. Though this was a short-lived opportunity for African American workers, it reveals much about their search for economic stability. The historian Peter Rachleff concludes that despite "their creativity and commitment, the Knights would disintegrate as rapidly as they arose."[53] Amid the mounting turmoil of political and social change in Richmond by the late nineteenth century, many of its black citizens remained focused on obtaining full equality.

Jones's parents were in the forefront of Richmond's black upper-class activity. Joseph Jones actively fought for black rights. In the early 1880s, he led one of the first successful fights to get black teachers in the "Negro" public schools of Richmond. He also conducted numerous debates in the "religious press of the community with a Catholic priest on the relative merits of Catholicism and Protestantism."[54] Eugene Kinckle Jones observed his parents "serving on mixed faculties of white and colored teachers in which equality was recognized within the group and where it was nothing strange to see highly educated northern white people sit at meals with similarly trained Negroes."[55] He claimed that such activities contributed to his belief that all men are created equal and, if given an opportunity, black men and women would measure up with "any other racial variety."[56]

While growing up in the old Confederate capitol in the 1880s and 1890s, Eugene Kinckle Jones enjoyed unique and enviable opportunities and experiences. He often saw blacks and whites intermingling as a result of his parents' professional status within the Jackson Ward community. This left an impression on young Eugene; few black youngsters would have experienced such interactions at the turn of the twentieth century. As a result of his childhood exposure, Jones developed a yearning for higher education. On numerous occasions he was treated to the unusual experience of observing students from Africa and the West Indies on "par with . . . our own Negro students" at Virginia Union and Hartshorn College. Jones also witnessed those same African American students leaving for northern institutions, not unlike his parents, and matching "their wits with the best young white minds of the North, [giving] a good account of themselves."[57]

Jones's early education was done in the black public schools of Richmond. Upon graduation from high school, Jones enrolled in Wayland Seminary, which merged with Virginia Union University of Richmond in 1899.[58] Few black institutions could match the education offered by Virginia Union at the turn of the century. It exemplified the classical education that was being offered in many American educational institutions. The school was comprised of three divisions, "an academy of preparatory instruction and manual crafts, a liberal arts college, and a theological department." All the classics were covered: Latin, Greek, Hebrew, French, and German; European and American history; science and mathematics; and, of course, the Bible. Booker T. Washington's industrial-educational model received little if any attention at the Virginia Union campus.[59] Richmond and Atlanta were the chief southern anti-Washington strongholds.[60] Virginia Union University and the *Planet* had been known to attack the Washington camp. Richmond sent representatives to the first meeting of the Niagara Movement in 1905.[61] The Niagara Movement meeting was called by W. E. B. DuBois at Buffalo, New York, to address the growing concerns after the 1896 *Plessy v. Ferguson* Supreme Court ruling, which rendered African Americans as second-class citizens in the eyes of the law. This type of activity began to fuel a new and younger generation of African Americans.

With Eugene Kinckle Jones's education complete in Richmond, he was prepared to match wits with the best young white minds of the North. In 1905 he graduated Virginia Union University and enrolled in Cornell University in Ithaca, New York. This northward trek was typical of the southern black aristocratic class at the turn of the century.[62] Most blacks who received advanced education prior to the late 1930s took their degrees in the North because there were no advanced-degree programs at black institutions in the South. Furthermore, no southern white institutions admitted blacks.[63] Perhaps Jones was able to attend Cornell due to the contacts his parents had secured during their tenure in the North while pursuing their own education during Reconstruction.

By the turn of the twentieth century, Cornell had an acceptable reputation as a liberal white institution among black intellectual circles. The philanthropist Henry W. Sage granted Cornell several generous amounts of money in 1885. By the 1890s, the university had become an educational institution of unusual financial security. The first endowed chairs at Cornell were in ethics and philosophy with a total sum of seventy thousand dollars. Again in 1890, Sage offered two hundred thousand dollars to open up the Susan Linn Sage School of Philosophy. The school and chairs were named for Sage's deceased wife (which occurred, coincidentally, the same month and year of Jones's birth, July 1885). Professor Walter F. Wilcox taught one of the school's most popular courses, social statistics.[64]

Jones spent half of his first year at Cornell studying civil engineering, a reflection of his love of mathematics. Eventually, Jones was convinced that a career in economics and social science would better enable him to serve black people. Perhaps Wilcox, an expert on Negro conditions who was empathetic toward black advancement, aided Jones in the decision to change his major. Wilcox convinced him that the job market in engineering would not be open to him because of his race; he arranged for Jones to enter graduate school and established the two-and-a-half-year time frame for its completion. Jones completed his studies at Cornell well within record time of the initial agreement. In the spring of 1908, he graduated with a master's degree in social science, focused on economics and sociology.[65]

Jones aligned himself with Professor Wilcox throughout his tenure as a student at Cornell. Wilcox was in his second decade with Cornell by the time Jones arrived in 1905. A specialist in political science and statistics, he belonged to an elite group of faculty members by the turn of the twentieth century. Wilcox eventually became one of the first on the faculty to be elected to the Board of Trustees in 1916; this was the first time an American university had allowed a faculty member to serve on its governing body. Other eastern schools followed what became known as the "Cornell idea."

Aside from meeting with the timetable established for his course of study, Jones took several of Wilcox's classes in ethics and social statistics, for which he conducted some of his first studies on racial statistics. While a student in 1907, Jones wrote to the most prominent black social scientist and historian in the United States, W. E. B. DuBois of Atlanta University, at Wilcox's instruction. He was given an assignment to justify through "representative men of the country" the reasoning for capitalizing the word "Negro." Jones wrote to DuBois: "The task I consented to perform for Prof. Wilcox is to secure all possible data, which one can consider authoritative, on the method pursued and the reasons given for so spelling the word by various writers."[66] He also disclosed to DuBois that he was a "Negro" student at Cornell studying toward a master's degree in social science and economics. This would be the beginning of a lasting relationship. Again in 1908, Jones wrote to DuBois requesting information concerning the "Health of the American Negro."[67]

When Jones arrived at Ithaca, he understood the nature of race relations in the South. He proclaimed: "A boy brought up as I was in the capital of the old Confederacy, Richmond, especially during the late 1880s and the 1890s, would have the factors involved in the problems of race indelibly impressed upon his mind."[68] Jones left Richmond to pursue advanced education at a time of entrenched racial hatred throughout the South and mounting racial discord throughout much of the North. The *Plessy v. Ferguson* decision had established legal segregation in the previous decade. Though the case directly addressed seating on railway lines, its implications eventually were felt in every aspect of American life. The writer Harvey Fireside laments that the 1896 case was "not just in railways but in schools, restaurants, hotels, theaters, and other areas of social life."[69] African Americans of every social and economic status had to reassess their acquired freedoms, even blacks of Jones's middle-class background. Jones stated in 1940, "Whites were asking further to proscribe Negroes by segregation, Jim Crow, and disfranchisement legislation."[70]

Jones also experienced Jim Crow proscriptions upon his arrival at Cornell. While the university admitted black students, it was not always a conducive environment for learning. Black students during this era were not permitted to live in campus housing or to take their meals among white students. Therefore, they had the added burden of living off campus. Most of the black student body boarded in the homes of Ithaca's black residents; Jones boarded at 214 Hazen Street.[71] The historian Charles Harris Wesley lamented that "the cleavage, characteristic of this period, had laid the basis for the division even in college life."[72] What Jones and his fellow black students found in Ithaca was a northern Jim Crow determined to limit the extent of their achievements. Carol Kammen's recent study, *Part and Apart: The Black Experience at Cornell, 1865–1945,* found that in general Cornell did not code its students' race. Whether Jones knew that his file was marked "Colored Student" is uncertain. The university coded the records of some but not all black students in this manner.[73]

The first decade of the twentieth century offered little hope for African Americans outside of the institutions that they built and fostered themselves. The Age of Jim Crow had come as a result of southern redemption and northern industrial expansion.[74] African Americans found themselves excluded or only marginally included in practically every aspect of American society—socially, economically, and politically. During the first decade of the new century, a plethora of black protest and advancement institutions were born out of necessity, espousing ideals of racial solidarity and self-help: The Negro Business League, founded in 1900; the National Afro-American Council, 1903; the National Association of Negro Teachers, 1903; the beginnings of the National Urban League, 1905; the National Association for the Advancement of Colored People, 1905 (through the Niagara Movement). These organizations were established for the purpose of securing African American social, economic, and political equality in an oppressive society. "Pressures of segregation, discrimination, mistreatment, prejudice, caste, and neglect of consideration were being exerted on the black people in many places, as they were endeavoring to advance and improve their status."[75] This was the twofold nature of a black student's experiences at Cornell University at the start of the twentieth century: though Jim Crow existed in the larger society, Jones and his peers were convinced of their abilities to make a difference through their chosen disciplines.

Black students at Cornell confronted considerable isolation during those dark days of segregation. There were so few black students enrolled at the time that they seldom encountered one another. Had it not been for Jim Crow exclusions from white fraternities, it is doubtful that black fraternities would have evolved at such a crucial point in time. Many blacks in education did not favor the development of black fraternities, but Jones failitated the establishment of the first black Greek-lettered fraternity in the United States, Alpha Phi Alpha, at Cornell in 1906. Henry Arthur Callis, a "jewel" or founding member of the fraternity, proclaimed, "Diversity rather than unity of background, interests, and objectives led these young men to Ithaca in 1905."[76]

Several of the young men involved in the establishment of Alpha Phi Alpha were from "moderately secure middle-class homes." Jones belonged to this group of Cornell students who expected employment upon graduation, "despite the handicap of race."[77] Seven young men were a part of this history-making event in Cornell's history: Henry Arthur Callis, physician; George Biddle Kelley, civil engineer; Charles Henry Chapman, educator; Nathaniel Allison Murray, educator; Vertner Woodson Tandy, architect; Robert Harold Ogle, federal service; and Eugene Kinckle Jones, social reformer. Most of these individuals had come from stable middle-class backgrounds from the upper South and Northeast; Tandy hailed from the border state of Kentucky. They came from families that had benefited from Reconstruction. Against the backdrop of a Jim Crow society that offered little opportunity for economic, social, and political mobility, the founding members of this fraternity offered each other a sense of camaraderie and sought to use the fraternity as a means of aiding the downtrodden black community. Callis declared, "Society offered us narrowly circumscribed opportunity and no security. Out of our need, our fraternity brought social purpose and social action."[78]

Jones was the first initiate of the fraternity in 1906. This gave him a dual place in its history, as a jewel and first initiate.[79] Jones and Callis wrote the fraternity's constitution together, and they remained close throughout their lives. Jones has been referred to as the "most dynamic and forceful" of the initial members. Jones and Callis had both witnessed the lecture on campus by Mary Church Terrell and had sat through Wilcox's class lectures, in which he had frequently quoted DuBois.[80] Wilcox and DuBois often spent summers together in Atlanta, researching and writing on the socioeconomic conditions of African Americans.[81] Such incidents aroused a level of awareness in these two students about the usefulness of studies in social science, government, and economics.

The following school year, in 1907, Jones was elected president of Alpha Phi Alpha, and under his administration the organization expanded its boundaries. Jones stated that he "personally organized the first two chapters in other colleges,"[82] at Howard University and Virginia Union, Jones's alma mater. It is likely that Callis played a major role in the efforts to establish the fraternity at Howard University, as he was enrolled there for medical school. At any rate, these young men followed historical precedent in keeping with the black-community traditions of mutual-aid and beneficial societies. Callis stated later in his life, "We were convinced that leadership in the struggle to overcome race prejudice in America depended upon college-trained young people. The talented tenth Dr. DuBois had heralded as the hope of the Negro American rather than the humble servitor prescribed by Booker T. Washington's program."[83] The historian Willard Gatewood contends that "in an age of rising expectations, they [blacks] encountered a degree of social segregation, political disfranchisement, educational discrimination, and economic exploitation experienced by no other segment of the American population."[84] Against this backdrop, young African Americans such as Jones and his peers at Cornell persevered.

Jones had demonstrated his abilities to his mentors and his leadership to his peers. In 1908, after graduation from Cornell University with a master's degree in economics and social science, Jones would have to put the ideals and motto of the new fraternity to work: "We shall be first of all, servants of all, we shall transcend all." Upon leaving Ithaca, Jones could only secure employment as a schoolteacher in private and public schools for blacks in Louisville, Kentucky.

On March 11, 1909, Jones married Blanche Ruby Watson of Richmond. She had also graduated from Virginia Union University. Out of this union, two children were born: Eugene Kinckle Jones Jr. and Adele Rosa Jones. In 1911, while the Jones children were still in infancy, Jones met Dr. George Edmund Haynes, an eminent black sociologist.[85] Haynes proposed that he come to New York and work for the newly formed League on Urban Conditions among Negroes. Jones's family name and academic preparations were preceding him. The noted minister Adam Clayton Powell Sr. responded to one inquiry, "[K]nowledge of the splendid family from which he comes and the two excellent institutions from which he graduated, coupled with his three years experience as a teacher at one of our southern schools, it seems to me that our faith becomes the substance of things hoped for. . . . Our problem in Harlem has been one that no one has been able to handle so far, but if I have any vote I will cast it in favor of experimenting with Mr. Jones."[86] New York would provide Jones with an opportunity to illustrate his ideas and philosophies concerning the social conditions of black life, eventually propelling him before a national and international audience. The time had arrived for him to test his capabilities and leadership style on the larger black community and ultimately to instruct and inform the nation of the social woes that confronted black America.

Rosa Kinckle Jones, mother of Eugene Kinckle Jones. (Kinckle Jones Family Collection)

Eugene Kinckle Jones ca. 1916, as he took over the helm at the NUL. (Kinckle Jones Family Collection)

(Left to right:) Joseph E. Jones, Eugene Kinckle Jones, and Eugene Kinckle Jones Jr. (Kinckle Jones Family Collection)

Sicily Jones's gravesite in Norwich, Connecticut. He was the Jones family patriarch. (Kinckle Jones Family Collection)

Joseph E. Jones, the father of Eugene Kinckle Jones Sr., as he joined the faculty of Virginia Union University ca. 1879. (Kinckle Jones Family Collection)

Blanche Watson Jones, wife of Eugene Kinckle Jones Sr. (Kinckle Jones
Family Collection)

Maggie L. Walker. (National Park Service, Maggie L. Walker
National Historic Site)

2. Building Alliances

The National Urban League has been particularly useful in its contribution towards the solution of the problem of races in the United States, because it has sought to secure the co-operation of leading people of both races in attacking these problems.
—President Warren G. Harding, 1921

Social work was going through a professional transformation by the 1920s. In 1915, Abraham Flexner, a representative of the Carnegie Foundation, informed social workers that they were not professionals due to their field's lack of a scientific methodology: "It lacks specificity of aim; social workers need to be well informed, well balanced, tactful, judicious, sympathetic, resourceful, but no definite kind or kinds of technical skills are needed."[1] It was to this end that most social workers sought to create a reputable body of knowledge. Social workers considered themselves to be professionals as early as 1921. In their urgency to counter Flexner's assessment, the American Association of Social Workers (AASW) was founded in that year. The organization was founded by white social workers to address their desire for professional status.

When white social workers served the poor and less fortunate (often black people), their efforts were viewed by many black social workers as charity that brought about little meaningful change. This perception is clear in an article written by Eugene Kinckle Jones as executive secretary of the National Urban League in a 1921 edition of *The Messenger*: "In case of white organizations interested more or less in Negro welfare, it has taken on the character of material aid given with no special desire to render the recipient independent but to relieve immediate suffering. This is especially true of many southern communities where the Charity Organization Society or the Associated Charities has maintained a list of indigent colored people who have received the weekly basket."[2]

Jones worked tirelessly to integrate the profession of social work. Social workers have always viewed themselves as part of a helping profession, ameliorating human woes, driven by ethical, humanistic, and social concerns, and therefore social work was always a dual profession: there was social work, the occupation, which at times was manipulated by persons with wealth and power to maintain some sense of social order.[3] And there were also numerous social workers who were motivated out of passion, altruism, and respect for the clients they served. Consequently, social workers saw themselves as a separate entity from other professions as providers of a distinct service.[4]

Though social workers received a major rejection from one of the nation's leading philanthropic societies, the Carnegie Foundation, in 1915, it was only the beginning of decades of changes that would eventually alter the social-work establishment. Some of the first social-work activities began within charity organizations in the late 1880s and into the 1890s. Much of the settlement-house movement came about as a means to aid European immigrants, mainly from southern and eastern Europe. Social-work activities of those early organizations were seen as community efforts to integrate the immigrants into the native white communities. Recent scholarship suggests that early social workers acted as agents of the middle class. This evolution can be seen as one of the many efforts to professionalize the occupation.[5] The social-work historian Clarke Chambers concludes, "[S]ocialized by formal training and practical experience to maintain social distance and to strive for objective analysis, social workers, longing for recognition as truly professional persons, were generally little inclined to engage themselves with issues of class, race, social power, and property. Social workers generally, in whatever era, did indeed so strongly reflect a prevailing middle-class ethos that only a few rare souls in any generation were able to transcend its limitations and bias."[6]

Black social workers were not afforded such luxuries. This set middle-class, white social workers apart from the concerns of the black social-work movement. Early white social-work activities sought to assimilate the recent white immigrant populace into mainstream American society. The numerous immigrants who poured into northern cities underscored the need for white social workers. White social workers dealt with class and gender issues, but they were reluctant to add the question of race to their agendas. Black social workers were always aware of the race question in all their efforts; at times they were consumed by the constant reminder of racial injustices.[7] Though black social workers were agents of the black middle class, they could not escape the insults of a Jim Crow society. Therefore, their accomplishments must be understood through the lens of a class system that existed within the American caste system of racism.

European immigration continued to swell until 1914, when Europe exploded with the First World War. From the start of the war through 1918, Europeans were no longer immigrating into the United States. European immigrants totaled 1,218,480 in 1914. The United States entered the war in 1917. According to the U.S. Census, by the last year of the war in 1918, European immigration totaled just over 110,000.[8] As a result of this decrease, northern cities began to attract southern black migrants. Black southerners began their northward trek with the outbreak of the war in Europe and continued this pattern of movement well after the war.

Northern white settlement houses did not embrace southern black new-comers.[9] When they did address the needs of African Americans, they were careful not to integrate their activities with those of the white residents. The historian Michael Katz contends that although Jane Addams, Edith Abbott, Sophonisba Breckenridge, and Florence Kelley are viewed as the left wing of the settlement-house movement, "[N]o differences separated them from their more openly racist colleagues."[10] They simply refused to "integrate their settlement houses. Even when the racial composition of their neighborhoods changed, most settlements remained white islands." Katz further claims that "the handful of settlements opened to serve blacks were always few, always separate, and always unequal."[11]

Florette Henri's *Black Migration* makes clear that black people had been moving in America from colonial times onward, "looking for freedom and opportunity." Black Americans were no different than other people; "they shared in the general American pattern of mobility." The first major migration to the North by southern blacks peaked between 1916 and 1918. Coupled with the wartime efforts, four major factors spurred black migrants:

1. Low wages in the South,
2. Mistreatment by whites,
3. Injustices and evils of tenant farming,
4. Increased dissatisfaction.[12]

Black southern migrants began arriving in the North as a result of industry's demand for labor as early as 1914, but World War I spurred the largest migration of African Americans from the American South in the history of the United States. Wartime sanctions against European immigration created a demand for southern black labor. Between 1915 and 1925, thousands of rural southern black people left family, friends, and extended families to head for "the Promised Land" in the North.[13]

There are numerous reasons that black people quit the South to live in the North. Between 1865 and 1914, black southerners migrated in comparatively small numbers to the North. This migratory pattern seemingly offered greater hope than previous migration patterns, especially for blacks from the deep South who left for Kansas and Oklahoma during the 1880s and 1890s.[14]

Migration was enticing at a time when the plight of black life throughout the South was dismal. By 1915, the boll weevil had made its way through the South. The infestation started in Mexico and quickly spread to the United States, destroying entire fields of cotton and sometimes farm animals.[15] In addition, mechanization established new forms of economic marginalization for blacks throughout nearly all of the southern United States.

The sociologist Carole Marks concludes that with new technology, "many jobs were redefined, and the stigma attached to them eroded." Marks further states that in numerous southern communities, newspaper editorials demanded that available jobs be given to whites first. One black migrant lamented, "The whites done taken all our men's jobs, they are street workers, scavengers, dump fillers, and everything. All white men got the jobs around the city hall that colored use[d] to have." He concluded, "back to the cotton fields, city jobs are for white folks."[16] The end of the Civil War had displaced many skilled blacks, and by the turn of the twentieth century, agrarian and unskilled blacks faced increasing competition from whites.[17]

Numerous northern industries took advantage of this opportunity to play upon the sentiments that existed among the south's black population. Many industries began sending agents into the South to recruit black workers. Newspapers became one of the greatest advocates of black migration, with ads that asked, "Why should the Negro stay in the South? West Indians live North." The *Chicago Defender* was known as the bearer of glad tidings to many southern blacks. Letters from friends and relatives already in the North became another source of advocacy. One sister living in Chicago wrote to another sister in the South, "My dear sister: I was agreeably surprised to hear from you and to hear from home. I am well and thankful to say I am doing well. The weather and everything else was a surprise to me when I came. . . . Tell your husband work is plentiful here and he won't have to loaf if he want to work. . . . I will send you a paper as soon as one come along[;] they send out extras two or three times a day."[18] Accessible railway lines provided easy access for blacks to move north. Railroads had proliferated immediately following the Civil War, and by the turn of the twentieth century, they were the predominant form of transportation in migration.

Recent scholarship has revealed specific black southern migration patterns from regions and/or states into distinct areas of the North. Because of the direct railroad lines, Chicago became the home of black southerners from Mississippi, Arkansas, Alabama, Louisiana, and Texas. The black population of New York increased due to migrants from North Carolina, South Carolina, Virginia, Georgia, and Alabama, with North Carolina contributing 20 percent of the total population. According to the National Advisory Commission on Civil Disorders in 1968, three distinct patterns of migration are evident: north along the Atlantic Seaboard toward Boston, from Mississippi toward Chicago, and west from Texas and Louisiana toward California.[19]

The Department of Commerce reported in 1935 that New York, Chicago, and Philadelphia had the largest black populations among northern cities. Between 1910 and 1920, the black population in New York increased from 91,709 to 152,467; Chicago from 44,103 to 109,453; and Philadelphia from 84,459 to 134,229. Since New York stood out as a black metropolis, more and more blacks sought to find their way there. By 1911, many large northern cities began to adopt well-defined lines of discrimination and segregation. In New York City, white property owners adopted restrictive covenants. Blacks experienced overcrowding in their housing conditions as a result of this act of discrimination.[20]

White homeowners in New York adopted and signed restrictive housing covenants in February 1911. These contractual agreements among white homeowners stipulated that they could not sell or lease property to blacks. When the 1917 Supreme Court ruled in *Buchanan v. Warley,* national newspaper headlines announced support for the court's decision to reject the covenants as unconstitutional. On November 6, 1917, the *New York Times* headline read: "Race Segregation Invalid." The article reported that "[c]ompulsory separation of the negro and white races in residential districts was a violation of the Constitution, the Supreme Court held in a unanimous opinion."[21]

The Supreme Court's decision in 1917 ruled the covenants as unconstitutional and in violation of the Fourteenth Amendment. However, in 1926 the high court ruled in *Corrigan v. Buckley* that the covenants were constitutional. White homeowners were able to win this victory because of their adoption of private agreements not to sell or rent their homes to nonwhites. In short, the courts granted white homeowners the right to restrict African Americans from all white neighborhoods.[22]

Many northern cities experienced an increased black migrant population, and this demographic transformation became a major concern for early social workers. In addition to mounting concerns about conditions in northern cities, social workers urgently desired increased professionalization, prompted by the growing needs of a society that was rapidly becoming more diverse. Black social workers sought the same levels of professional development as their white counterparts.

In the tumultuous context of the early twentieth century, social workers were faced with the dual challenge of adjusting their tactics to meet the growing needs of a black migrant population and establishing themselves as professionals. It proved to be a time of rapid change—an age of progress, and an age of great turmoil. Numerous race riots erupted in cities across the nation early in the twentieth century. The race riots of the 1910s set the social tone for race relations, and by the 1920s, mounting tensions were an established social reality for most black urban dwellers. Many northern cities erupted in racial chaos by the turn of the twentieth century: Springfield, Illinois, in 1908; East St. Louis, Illinois, in 1917; Chicago in 1919; and Tulsa, Oklahoma, in 1921.[23]

Ultimately, the duties of black social workers and the aims of the NUL included evaluating and reviewing settlement houses, in addition to other specific concerns of migrating blacks. Black social workers dealt with employment bureaus for juveniles and adults. They also helped negotiate contracts for black workers and placed workers in industrial plants and generally tried to increase the level of black employment. Many migrants were ill-prepared for their new lives in the North. Therefore, black social workers also paid attention to health-care concerns and provided guidance in home economics to families that needed assistance in arranging budgets and preparing nutritious food. Jones and other black social workers often found these duties time-consuming and exhausting.

When Jones arrived in New York City in 1911 to accept the position of field secretary of the League on Urban Conditions among Negroes, renamed National Urban League in 1920, his energies were engaged on several fronts. He became an advocate for black migrants, and he also sought to secure the black social worker's legitimation as a professional. His first major undertaking was to assess the conditions of black life in the inner city of New York and to submit a report to NUL officials. As a result of that first assessment, Jones and George E. Haynes presented the following principles as the basis for the foundation of the NUL:

1. To bring about coordination and cooperation among existing agencies and organizations for improving the industrial, economic, and social conditions of Negroes and to develop other agencies and organizations, where necessary.
2. To secure and train Negro social workers.
3. To make studies of the industrial, economic, and social conditions among Negroes.
4. To promote, encourage, assist, and engage in any and all kinds of work for improving the industrial, economic, and social conditions among Negroes.[24]

Several duties were essential to Jones's task of assisting new migrants with their acclimation to the urban environment. He often met new arrivals at the train depot, then assisted them in finding housing and employment. He discussed expanded employment opportunities with industry and business leaders. Many companies were only willing to hire blacks for menial jobs, and often as strikebreakers.

Recognizing the shortage of laborers and time, Jones and other black social workers set out to convince white social workers of the need to address the race question. By 1921, Jones had begun working to unify the missions of black and white social workers. In his 1921 article in *The Messenger,* Jones argued: "As soon as possible efforts should be made to prevent the organization of movements to care only for colored people. Where possible, white organizations should be induced to include Negroes in their programs . . . and to employ colored workers to handle their cases." This statement illuminates part of Jones's mission as a social worker. The plan of action that he devised for black social workers to some degree defied the meaning of professions. According to Magali Larson's model in *The Rise of Professionalism: A Sociological Analysis* (1977), professionals were to prosper economically through their clients. In this instance, black social workers were fighting an enormous uphill battle. Their clients usually had not prospered economically. The National Conference of Social Work began to address the issues facing African American clientele at its 1923 meeting. During this meeting, a social worker "pointed out that one rarely finds white people even in an audience of social workers, with their efforts to put themselves in the other fellow's place." The social-work scholar David Fogel concluded, "[B]efore a caseworker could identify with a client, he would have to be adequately aware of the real problems affecting his client."[25] White social workers discovered in 1923 what many black social workers were already aware of.

Early in his brief tenure as the first executive director, the NUL's cofounder George Edmund Haynes made some initial attempts to create professional training schools for black social workers in the South. Shortly after Haynes helped establish the NUL in 1910,[26] he left for Nashville, Tennessee, to join the faculty at Fisk University. Haynes was present at the initial meeting with Frances A. Kellor and Ruth Standish Baldwin at which the NUL was founded; Baldwin went on to become the major benefactor of the Urban League. Her husband, William H. Baldwin, had recently died, and she was left with an enormous financial estate.[27] The social-work scholar Iris Carlton-LaNey found that Haynes believed "that securing and training African American social workers for service in urban communities was the most pressing need of the newly established National League on Urban Conditions Among Negroes (NUL)."[28]

Soon after arriving at Fisk, Haynes established the first social-work training department in the country for African Americans. He insisted on a core curriculum for social-work training. Courses included Elementary Economics: Principles and Organization; Advanced Economics: Economics and Labor Problems; Sociology and Social Problems; and History of the Negro in America and the Negro Problem. Haynes believed that an understanding of black history was essential to understanding and improving the social conditions of black people.[29] The social-work historian Clarke Chambers concluded that the first three decades of the twentieth century were the "seedtime of reform." Chambers describes the period from 1918 to 1933 as an era when social reformers were largely dealing with trial and error.[30] Between the end of World War I and the New Deal, social reformers reacted to events rather than taking preventive actions. Social-work activity was still loyal to the community-chest concept, which offered temporary relief rather than permanent solutions. "Theoretically settlements still functioned as organizers for their neighborhoods."[31]

Black social workers were engaging in several other activities to accomplish their goals of becoming professionals in the early twentieth century. In 1915, the first black social-work organization was established in New York City, the Social Workers' Club. Jones, as president of the club, wrote to W. E. B. DuBois in 1918, inviting him to join. DuBois wrote back on April 10, 1918, stating that he would be "glad to join the Social Workers' Club, but I am afraid that I shall not often have the pleasure of attending meetings."[32] By 1918 the organization boasted a roaster of eighty members and proclaimed as its object: "To furnish means of friendly intercourse between members of the profession." It is interesting to note that most of those who considered themselves social workers were not necessarily trained in the traditional manner. Accompanying Jones as officers of the Social Workers' Club in 1918 were Mrs. C. L. Anderson, vice president; Carita V. Owens, secretary; and Adah B. Thoms, treasurer.[33] Black social workers in general were actively involved in the professionalization process, although mainstream social-work histories often do not reveal their participation. The social-work scholars Robenia Baker Gary and Lawrence E. Gary note that black social workers were busy creating similar kinds of activities as those of their white counterparts. They too participated in "demonstration to the public that everybody 'with love in his heart' could not do social work in a professional manner; identification of knowledge and skills necessary for the practice of social work; the establishment of schools for the training of social worker; the development of professional organizations; the publication of major books dealing with social work theory and practice; the development of professional journals; and an identification of values shared by social workers."[34]

Most black social workers in the early twentieth century were trained at black colleges. Fisk offered the only undergraduate program in the country that catered to black people in the first three decades of the twentieth century. However, by the mid-1920s two southern black institutions had established graduate training for black social workers: the Atlanta University School of Social Work, organized in 1920, and the Bishop Tuttle School at Raleigh, North Carolina, established in 1925.[35] Fisk University was established in 1865 at Nashville, and it soon became the darling of the American Missionary Association. The university was named for General Clinton B. Fisk, the assistant commissioner of the Freedmen's Bureau of Tennessee and Kentucky, in honor of his generous donations and loyal support to the institution during its infancy. W. E. B. DuBois remarked many years later, "[T]he aim in founding Fisk and similar schools . . . was to maintain the standards of lower training by giving leaders and teachers the best possible instruction, and more important, to furnish blacks with adequate standards of human culture and lofty ideals of life." Geographically, Fisk served as a convenient location for training both northern and southern black social workers.[36]

Eugene Kinckle Jones is largely responsible for the first successful approach to the problem of how to provide professional training to black social workers. The training institutes were all established at white educational institutions.[37] Jones's first step toward assisting with the black social workers' plight was to broaden educational opportunities. He sought to educate a pool of black social workers by providing fellowships for young black college graduates or persons who at least expressed a definite interest in social work.

Throughout *Opportunity,* the NUL's magazine designed in 1923 to promote literary and other concerns of the Urban League and the black community at large, advertisements encouraged interested persons to take advantage of these fellowships. In Jones's annual report of the accomplishments of the NUL for 1922, he wrote specifically of the training of black social workers. At the close of the school year 1921–22, he stated that two of the NUL's fellows had completed their training at the New York School of Social Work and the Carnegie School of Technology at the University of Pittsburgh. The two individuals in question found employment, one in family casework in Minneapolis, and the other with a branch of the YWCA.

In 1910, when Jones began working with the NUL, securing social-work fellowships was already considered an integral part of its overall mission. This was at a time when social-service programs were practically unknown

to black people, and there were few black workers to carry out these programs. Haynes was responsible for bringing this idea of training black social
workers to the NUL at its inception. Soon after Jones joined its staff, the
NUL incorporated its first plan, which would allow for two fellowships to be
offered at the New York School of Social Work. A generous grant from the
Carnegie Foundation in 1923 expanded the system to include such institutions as the Graduate School of Social Administration at the University of
Chicago, the Carnegie School of Technology at the University of Pittsburgh,
Simmons College of Boston, and the Pennsylvania School of Social Work in
Philadelphia.[38] It remains unclear whether these schools all maintained the
level of commitment that the New York School of Social Work did.

The New York School of Social Work first offered classes in the summer of
1898, and by the 1920s it was the leading program of graduate studies offering
the one-year advanced degree in social work. In addition to the fellowships,
the NUL took on the responsibility of field-training individuals in the areas
of health-care concerns, housing, industry, and recreation.[39] Usually after
three to six months, they were placed in responsible positions. Jones and the
NUL felt that the field training underscored the value of special training for
social workers and contributed to professionalizing the occupation.

One southern black school took an active role in the training of black
social workers starting in 1910. Immediately upon Haynes's arrival at Fisk
University in 1910, he implemented a program to address black social work.
According to Joe M. Richardson, "Under the leadership of Haynes and
[President] McKenzie many new friends were enlisted in the cause of social
betterment of Nashville." Atlanta University's School of Social Work was
established in 1920 to train graduate students. Fisk University had the only
well-established school of social-work training for blacks, offering the bac-
calaureate degree. According to Francis Kornegay, retired executive director
of the Detroit Urban League, Atlanta University's graduate program taught
only a few courses in sociology at this time. Haynes assumed his position
at Fisk full-time in 1916, making it the only program in the country at the
time for African Americans. Jones was then appointed executive secretary
of the NUL. Jones and Haynes worked tirelessly to keep a pool of students
enrolled in the department at Fisk to eventually do the duties of social work
in the North and South.[40]

By 1923, a small pool of black social workers had been trained under the
auspices of Jones and the NUL. This body began immediately to combat
the exclusionary and discriminatory practices of white social-workers. The
National Conference of Social Workers was the umbrella organization that
supposedly brought all social workers together annually. In 1923, the NCSW

convened in Washington, D.C. According to the *Opportunity* editorial, there were six thousand delegates in attendance, including only seventy-five blacks. This meeting reportedly gave attention to the "Negro Problems." Among the black speakers were Jones, Gertrude McDougald, R. R. Moton, and Charles S. Johnson. Jones delivered a paper, "The Negro's Struggle for Health," in which he discussed African Americans' ability to combat certain types of diseases during slavery because they had come from the tropical zones of Africa. Jones stressed grave concern over whether black people would be able to withstand the diseases that plagued the crowded slums of northern cities. The health of African Americans was a subject Jones had long been interested in; his first writings on this subject are found in his correspondence with DuBois while a student at Cornell.[41] In spite of this grave concern, Jones expressed some optimism about the growing educational facilities throughout the South and the fact that blacks were still migrating north, "within the zone of better living conditions."[42] Although conditions were growing worse in the North, Jones felt that the region offered African Americans greater opportunities.

Several issues were addressed at the conference in 1923 concerning the "Negro Question." Black people's health, special problems of vocational guidance for black children, and the role of public opinion and relations were stressed. Jones participated in the section on public opinion of the NCSW, and he played a major role in planning the program. Black social workers were disappointed that once again no black person would be elected to its executive board. Some conference officials expressed an interest in electing a black social worker to the executive board, but this faction was viewed as radical. Black social workers were hoping that Washington, D.C., would be the conference site to secure this feat. The Nominating Committee nominated two black social workers, but the vote was defeated.

Jones was elected treasurer at the 1925 meeting in Cleveland. That meeting was also marked by black social workers' disapproval of a southern city for the 1926 meeting. They objected to Chattanooga, Tennessee, because not all delegates would be guaranteed the same privileges and accommodations. Chattanooga was thus forced out of the bid, giving way to Des Moines, Iowa. It can be assumed that African Americans serving in positions of power were influential in the decision. In 1925, Jones was elected to the Executive Committee of the conference, and Jesse O. Thomas, Forrester B. Washington, George E. Haynes, and Charles S. Johnson were elected as members of their division committees.[43]

Jones's efforts on behalf of black social workers made him one of the prominent social workers in America. He was the first African American elected to the Executive Committee of the NCSW in 1925. In the mid-1920s, the NUL had begun conducting investigations of living conditions among African Americans in urban centers, in keeping with the recently adopted scientific approaches of the NCSW.[44] Jones continued to address the "Problem of the Negro" throughout the 1920s. The NCSW provided a national, integrated audience for discussing racial issues and how black social workers could address them. Jones became a regular speaker at NCSW meetings. At the 1928 meeting in Memphis, he gave a paper on "Some Fundamental Factors in Regard to the Health of the Negro,"[45] and at the 1929 San Francisco meeting he spoke on "The Negro in Community Life."[46] Jones viewed himself and other black social workers involved in the NCSW "as messengers of good will from the colored people in an effort to improve interracial relationships." By the late 1920s, the NUL claimed that there had been "progress . . . in the field of social work for Negroes,"[47] undoubtedly due to the efforts of Jones and his colleagues.

Housing problems were of major concern to Jones and many of the local branches of the NUL in the 1920s. Black migration was at its peak, which created major housing problems for the New York City Urban League branch and those in other northern cities. The NUL complained to the governor of New York that the "Negro population was receiving less consideration than any other group."[48] In 1926, the NUL began its Better Housing campaign. The league sought the support of John D. Rockefeller Jr. for this campaign and eventually convinced him to purchase "a whole block in north Harlem." The New York campaign sparked interest within branches across the United States: Milwaukee, Detroit, Kansas City, Los Angeles, Philadelphia, St. Louis, Louisville, and Columbus are among the cities mentioned in a 1926 NUL report. The efforts of the Urban League in New York were believed by its supporters to eventually "have [had] a direct effect on Negro housing in cities throughout America and on the consideration given the Negro population in social reform."[49]

By 1926, Jones had achieved considerable recognition outside the social-work profession. Mayor James E. Walker of New York appointed five hundred representatives to serve on a nonpartisan committee to survey the city and plan for its future needs; eleven were black men. According to *Opportunity,* in addition to Jones, W. E. B. DuBois, James Weldon Johnson, Ferdinand Q. Moton, and John E. Nail were involved. Jones's reputation by 1928 had reached international proportions. He proclaimed, "In 1928 I attended the International Conference of Social Work in Paris as an American delegate; also the International Conference on Human Relations in Industry at Girton College, Cambridge, England." Jones also stated, "I believe very strongly that most of the acts of man are influenced by his economic outlook on life."[50]

Black people had begun to feel the sting of economic devastation in spite of their northward trek long before the Great Crash of 1929, and Jones had already begun to assist in their economic outlook. He worked diligently to overturn unjust woes brought on by the larger society.[51] Black social workers were always aware of the "race question" in all their efforts. White social workers dealt with class and gender, but they were reluctant to add race to their agendas, while black social workers experienced racial slights on a daily basis. The historian Elisabeth Lasch-Quinn argues that perhaps the greatest failure of the American settlement-house reform movement occurred at the crucial juncture of race.[52] The historian Michael Katz argues that even "the more liberal settlement leaders advocated economic and political equality, but not social equality."[53] Most white settlement-house workers did not support racial integration of their missions.

It was at this crucial juncture that the greatest need for black social workers found unwavering support through numerous advocates. Jones is an example of the tenacity that black social workers brought to their jobs in confronting the social woes of the black community. His support base was secured through a cadre of well-trained individuals, black and white, representing numerous fields of training. Jones stated late in his life, "I have always cultivated the friendship of Negro and white persons in key positions wherever it was my good fortune to meet them; and many educators, statesman, religious leaders, businessmen, and social workers have aided the cause I have espoused." During the 1920s, Jones was able to align himself with key philanthropic organizations to maintain the stability of the NUL. In spite of their many accomplishments, perhaps the greatest challenge to Jones, the NUL, and black social work remained before them, as they sought to define the meaning of professionalism and to build an institution of agency.

3. An Era of National Conflict and Cooperation

The opportunity for statesmanship service to humanity is ours. The obligation is ours. We cannot pass on to posterity the responsibility for work, which we should assume. The challenge of democracy is before us. The Negro is probably the real test of democracy in America.

—Eugene Kinckle Jones, 1925

The 1920s and 1930s proved to be busy for Jones, as his schedule kept him quite mobile. As the national spokesperson for the NUL, he found his duties ever expanding. The 1920s were a decade of constantly changing climates—politically, socially, and economically—for African Americans throughout American society. In spite of the major cultural awakening in black America through the Harlem Renaissance in the 1920s, many African Americans found their economic and political status dismal at best. Many African Americans who migrated from the oppressive South found racial discrimination in housing, jobs, and education mounting in the North. In 1929 they were hard hit by the Great Depression, which deepened their economic dislocation. In the midst of these economic hard times, Jones was fighting to further the goals of the NUL. The task of making sure that the NUL was adequately funded was his primary responsibility. He was therefore forced to make every use of his available financial and human resources. No doubt this was the greatest challenge of his career with the NUL. It was a continuing issue, as Jones noted in 1940 that many white philanthropists had been stingy with their giving during the Depression. The NUL received some of its operating funds through such philanthropists as the Rockefeller Foundation, the Julius Rosenwald Fund, and the Carnegie Foundation. Jones noted to Gunnar Myrdal in 1940 that even those leading philanthropists "will give small sums to Negro causes seemingly as balm to their consciences. They frequently will give to *one* Negro cause only as evidence of their 'interest in the Negro' while contributing to as many different white organizations as are represented by phases of social work in which they are interested."[1] The continual need to address the financial concerns of the NUL were mounting even before the 1920s. It was Jones's task from the time he joined the Urban League in 1911 to prove annually the worth of the organization to various philanthropic societies. After his appointment in 1916, it became the sole responsibility of the executive secretary.

As the recently appointed chief executive of the NUL, Jones's time and energy in the 1920s were also engaged in the infant social-work profession. Coupled with the demanding duties of the day-to-day operations of the NUL, Jones maintained a busy schedule of appointments and appearances around the country on behalf of the Urban League and its programs. This was also the decade in which the NUL laid the foundation for its identity among prominent American institutions, and Jones, as executive secretary, more than anyone else personified that identity. An editorial in the *New York Times* asserted that "[t]he name The National Urban League does not convey to many the purpose of this organization. But when it is known that KINCKLE JONES is its administrative secretary, its identity is better recognized."[2] Jones's conservative nature and no-nonsense approach to dealing with the social problems confronting black Americans were often unmatched. One scholar contends that most of the NUL's original mandate had gone unfulfilled during its first decade. The Urban League did not become a viable national organization until the advent of the First World War and the Great Migration.[3] Jones became executive secretary, and the public face of the NUL, at this time.

Jones was able to cultivate the national image of the Urban League through a host of activities. He represented the NUL with a very conservative approach; he was soft-spoken and nonconfrontational. He quickly became noted as a handsome, refined, and skillful leader. His activities included radio broadcasts, commencement speeches, addresses to local branches, aiding ventures such as the Durham Fact-Finding Conference, and the NUL's committee on race relations, which "suggested arguments to use in appealing to employers for jobs for Negroes." He worked also to establish cooperative relations with philanthropic organizations. Regardless of the occasion, Jones always found a way to highlight the most recent accomplishments of the NUL, along with the continual need for black social workers.

Though he involved himself with countless social matters, Jones's focus remained on social work for and by black people. In the midst of promoting the NUL as a major social-work institution in American society, he worked on numerous fronts with many leading black and white intellectuals. In the fall

of 1920, Jones submitted an important proposal to the Carnegie Foundation
on behalf of the NUL to secure funding for the creation of a Department of
Research and Investigations. This led to his first encounter with the historian
Carter G. Woodson, the founder of the Association for the Study of Afro-
American Life and History (ASALH) in 1915. Woodson and Monroe Work
of Tuskegee Institute had submitted to the Carnegie Foundation competing
proposals. Woodson was soliciting funds for the recently established ASALH,
and Work for ongoing efforts at Tuskegee Institute.[4] Although Jones, Woodson, and Work were initially unaware of each other's works, they were each
promptly informed by Carnegie officials of the others' proposals.

Carnegie Foundation officials were hoping to convince the three to agree to
some kind of joint venture. James R. Angell, the president of the foundation,
was aware that the proposals of Jones and Work were in direct competition
with each other, but he believed that a compromise could be reached. Though
evidence suggests that Jones and Work may have reached an agreement,
ironically, Woodson proved to be the holdout, declining to cooperate on
a joint project because of his long-standing personal distrust of Monroe
Work. Evidence is not conclusive as to the reason for their feud. However,
despite Woodson's reluctance to cooperate, in May 1921 the yearlong battle
was resolved, and the Carnegie Foundation decided to fund each of the three
proposals. Jones received his request with no stipulations.[5]

The Carnegie funds were used to help establish the research division of the
NUL, which would be devoted to the fellowship program and the publication of *Opportunity*. The Carnegie Foundation awarded Jones and the NUL
eight thousand dollars per year for five and a half years in 1921.[6] By this time,
the fellowship program was well under way, and by 1923 Jones had invited
the sociologist Charles S. Johnson to head the Department of Research and
Investigations of the NUL. Johnson had published his seminal work on the
infamous Chicago race riot of 1919, *The Negro in Chicago: A Study of Race
and a Race Riot,* in 1922. In addition to heading the division, he was editor
of *Opportunity* from 1923 to 1928, until he left to chair the Department of
Social Science at Fisk University. Johnson's name was most associated with
the magazine during this early period of its existence. The print voice of the
Urban League and its activities, *Opportunity* was a major factor in the literary
life of black America during the 1920s and 1930s.

The Harlem Renaissance movement of the 1920s was a social and cultural
revolution in black American arts and letters, and many Harlem Renaissance
personalities were first published in *Opportunity*. Through the magazine,
the NUL promoted the fellowship programs and the works of many Harlem
Renaissance writers and artists.[7] *Opportunity* was more than just a magazine;

it was a major journal. Unlike *The Crisis,* its only rival, it sought to promote labor and socioeconomic concerns. *The Crisis,* published by the NAACP, with DuBois as its editor-in-chief, was much more radical in content.[8]

One of the important consequences of the Carnegie funding was that it aided the establishment of the NUL's fellowships in social-work education. The longing for professional status and recognition by black social workers was never more intense than during the decade of the 1920s. Jones's efforts and those of the NUL collectively were well thought-out and systematically strategized during this process of evolutionary change. While Jones carefully orchestrated procedures through the NUL, his connections to a pool of well-trained black men helped to further his efforts. The sociologists Charles S. Johnson, Lawrence A. Oxley, Forrester B. Washington, T. Arnold Hill, E. Franklin Frazier, and George Edmund Haynes had studied at some of the finest schools in the country, including the University of Chicago and Columbia University. Practically all of them were well versed in sociology and social services. Frazier and Washington were only a few of the individuals who gained prominence in the field of social welfare for black people. They owed some credit for their education to the fellowship programs organized by the NUL under Jones's leadership.[9]

Several fellows rose to national prominence following their work with the Urban League: Ira D. Reid, E. Franklin Frazier, and Walter B. Chivers devoted the major portion of their careers to the teaching of sociology and to developing source materials through research. They each also did consulting at black colleges. Reid, Frazier, and Chivers eventually went on to chair departments of sociology at Atlanta University, Howard University, and Morehouse College in Atlanta, respectively. Their labors increased the pool of young black social workers. Much of the work pertaining to black social-work education has gone practically unnoticed in general social-work histories.[10]

The historian Ruth Hutchinson Crocker contends that "Jane Addams and Hull-House have overshadowed the history of the settlement movement in the United States."[11] Numerous black women had been working hard at relieving the social woes of the black community, and they were available for Jones's cause. For example, Fannie Barrier Williams made substantial progress in Chicago as early as 1904.[12] She founded the first successful settlement house in the country for black people in the city of Chicago. Black women contributed greatly to the relief of the woes suffered by black urban people and to the knowledge base that influenced succeeding generations of sociologists. Carlton-LaNey asserts that Elizabeth Ross Haynes, the wife of Dr. George Edmund Haynes whose professional career spanned from 1908 to 1940, was "an African American reformer of womanish consciousness" who championed "the rights of the African American race and . . . the rights of women."[13]

A number of black women devoted their careers to social work. A new and exciting interest had arisen in sociology by the early twentieth century, "particularly the study of Blacks, [which] also gave rise to a demand for college-trained social scientists. A disproportionate number of these were Black women as well."[14] Williams and numerous other black female social workers have been overlooked largely due to the double standards of race and sex in the 1920s. Black settlement-house work was overwhelmingly conducted by black women. Jane Edna Hunter of Cleveland established the Phillis Wheatley Association in 1913; W. Gertrude Brown headed the Phyllis Wheatley House of Minneapolis from 1924 to 1937; Birdye H. Haynes was head resident of the Wendell Phillips Settlement on the West Side of Chicago in 1909, until she moved to the Lincoln House in New York City.[15]

The historian Cynthia Neverdon-Morton argues that in many of the programs that were implemented by national organizations such as the NUL, black women did the duties, while the leadership roles remained dominated by men: "[T]his less glamorous but equally crucial work by women has gone largely unnoticed by historians."[16] The administrative duties in social work were almost always assigned to men, but the actual leadership roles that were often carried out by women are obscured. The social-work scholar Daniel J. Walkowitz concludes that the scientific model of the 1920s created tensions for female social workers. Objectivity and rationality were thought to be characteristics of male professionals, and women had to navigate a tightrope in order to "develop a work identity that would both give them professional status and preserve their femininity."[17] Coupled with the desire for professionalization, women social workers responded to the new expectations of professionalism. Moreover, women in the profession "found achievements illusory and problematic."[18] Carlton-LaNey argues that "racism and segregation placed strict limitations on what Birdye Henrietta Haynes . . . was able to accomplish during her social work career."[19] She worked in isolation from social-work colleagues and therefore was always overworked. Chambers insists that as historians begin to pay close "attention to the work of prominent and powerful men . . . they must also reckon with women who moved into positions of leadership, of local and national influence in charities and hospital social work."[20] The social-welfare scholar Cheryl D. Cromwell concludes that "the contributions of . . . Black women . . . are seldom, if ever, mentioned in the traditional social welfare or even Black History textbooks."[21] The social-work scholar Audreye E. Johnson concludes that "ignoring [black women's] myriad contributions is indeed a sin."[22]

Typically, neither black women nor men were chronicled in the list of prominent social-welfare pioneers in the period from 1890 to 1930. The medical historian Vanessa Northington Gamble discovered that "most of the records of black hospitals had been lost or destroyed."[23] This is true of other institutions that black men and women served as social workers and reformers; the fact that few records have survived contributes to these people's invisibility. With the exception of the NUL, the records of institutions such as the black settlement homes, black hospitals, black schools, and a host of others have not survived. Recent scholarship suggests that middle-class white women's realities tended to dominate progressive ideology. As the historian William Chafe points out, "Progressive white women failed even to consider the plight of their black sisters—even the more affluent among them."[24] This is echoed by Carlton-LaNey:

> If these white feminist reformers [Florence Kelley and Lillian Wald] could show such concern and caring for each other, why were they unable to recognize the stress under which Haynes labored and to embrace her similarly? Perhaps these reformers, ahead of their time in so many ways, were very much a part of their time in other ways. Adhering to the tenets of racial segregation that dictated both physical and social distance prevented these women from seeing the struggles of black women. Perhaps the noted antilynching crusader and journalist Ida Wells-Barnett was correct in her accusation that white reformers had an inability to "know the souls of Black women."[25]

Jones persisted with the education of a pool of black social workers, male and female.[26] An examination of his work and contributions in social work may suggest an answer to the historian William H. Chafe's query: "How do we integrate those male progressives who focused on social justice issues into this gender-based framework?"[27] Jones reached out to a much broader pool of constituents in his quest to fulfill this major void of available black social workers.

Jones kept abreast of current literature by and about African Americans, studying the works of such scholars as Carter G. Woodson. Though Woodson was a leading intellectual, other black intellectuals occasionally found him and his work unsettling. The historian Arvarh Strickland has stated that "various individuals described him as 'arrogant,' 'cantankerous,' and 'domineering.'"[28] Jones appears to have only engaged with Woodson intellectually. When Woodson's book, *The Negro in Our History*, was published in 1922, Jones rushed to review it. He noted that the book had several "handsome photographs and old prints." However, he questioned whether miscegenation and fornication should have been discussed so freely: "[Woodson's] brief treatment of subjects such as miscegenation and fornication . . . in the judgement of some will be considered a little too salacious for the youthful mind."[29] Perhaps due to Jones's reserved nature, he felt that such inclusions were in poor taste. In spite of this, Jones believed that "the publication meets a long felt need for a simple presentation of the relation which Negro life in America has borne to many of our country's important historical facts."[30]

Jones was not alone in questioning the "miscegenation and fornication" issue. His longtime intellectual and personal friend Arthur A. Schomburg offered some of the most biting criticism of Woodson's book. Schomburg's biographer, Elinor DesVerney Sinnette, suggests that his criticisms may have arisen from the fact that Woodson did not mention him in the acknowledgments. Many of the "handsome photographs and old prints" that Jones mentioned were loaned to Woodson from Schomburg's extensive personal collection of black history. Woodson and Schomburg continued their feud over the next few years until the New York Public Library purchased the Schomburg Collection in 1927. Woodson eventually acknowledged the importance of Schomburg's contributions to the study of black history when he proclaimed the sale "the outstanding event of the year."[31]

Jones played a greater role in the black intellectual movement of the 1920s than is generally acknowledged by most scholars. He was perhaps the most instrumental participant in helping establish a permanent repository for Schomburg's collection of black history. In 1926, Schomburg approached Jones, the NUL president L. Hollingsworth Wood, and Charles S. Johnson, the editor of *Opportunity*, to discuss turning over his massive collection of black memorabilia to the NUL. Schomburg was informed that the NUL was not in a position to take on such a collection, nor could their facilities accommodate the project. Jones, along with Wood and the director of the New York Public Library, Edwin H. Anderson, decided to approach the Carnegie Foundation, which agreed to purchase the collection in March 1926 for ten thousand dollars.[32] A year later, the 135th Street Branch of the New York Public Library received the collection.

In later years, Jones worked with Schomburg and a group of other notable intellectuals to cofound the Associates in Negro Folk Education in New York City and Atlanta. The organization published the Bronze Booklet Series from 1935 to 1938, which chronicled African American history in the people's own words. Membership included such individuals as Charles S. Johnson, Mary McLeod Bethune, Franklin Hopper, and Lyman Bryson of Teachers' College, Columbia University.[33]

Jones maintained a list of philanthropic organizations and frequently called upon the officers of such institutions as the Laura Spelman Rockefeller Memorial, the Carnegie Foundation of New York, the Friends of Mrs. Ella Sachs Plotz, the estate of Mrs. L. Hollingsworth Wood, and the Phelps Stokes Fund. In addition to these organizations, Jones helped persuade educational institutions to provide opportunities for black men and women to matriculate in social-work programs, including the New York School of Social Work, the Graduate School of Social Administration at the University of Chicago, the University of Pittsburgh, and Ohio State University. In addition to the financial concerns of the Urban League and its agenda, Jones was always promoting the continual training of black social workers.[34]

Jones sought to take advantage of every available means to further his mission. He appealed directly to the masses of black people with his self-help message through the use of the recently invented radio. On May 16, 1926, Jones delivered over the radio station WMCA at Hotel McAlpin in New York an address entitled "Go to High School, Go to College." The broadcast was sponsored by Alpha Phi Alpha Fraternity to encourage young African American students "to continue their education in high schools and in college." This provided an opportunity for Jones to inform young African Americans of the numerous options that awaited them if they pursued education. He also claimed in this address that "the past ten years have proved to be the banner period of this age." Perhaps to overshadow recent race riots and the economic dislocation African Americans suffered after World War I, he overstated the accomplishments of the race. But in spite of African Americans' many accomplishments, there were some bleak areas. Jones nevertheless declared, "Competent teachers, social workers, clergymen, and other community leaders are far too few in numbers, and should be augmented from the ranks of the Negro students of today." He took it upon himself to promote social work to and for African Americans, lobbying for an expansion of secondary and collegiate institutions. Furthermore, according to Jones, "the more liberal support of organizations working to secure larger civic and industrial opportunities for the Negro like the National Association for the Advancement of Colored People and the National Urban League" were reasons enough for young people to aspire. The fraternity was useful in expressing such issues of national interest within the black community.[35] Jones and Alpha Phi Alpha aided the cause of black America and supported its ideals of community uplift.

By the mid-1920s, Jones had achieved national prominence, and his speaking engagements had grown beyond strictly social-work audiences. In 1924, Virginia Union University awarded him the honorary degree of LLD. Jones remained one of Virginia Union's most distinguished alumni. He never broke ties with the university nor the city of Richmond.[36] In June 1926, he delivered the commencement address at West Virginia Collegiate Institute. "The Negro's Opportunity Today" was the title of his speech, in which he read a "who's who" list of African Americans. Never failing to include the accomplishments of black social workers and their contributions to society, he proclaimed, in a self-referential note: "A colored man is member of the National Conference of Social Work elected to this board of fifteen persons by a membership of four thousand social workers, the overwhelming majority of whom are white."[37] (Jones had been elected the previous year to the Executive Board of the NCSW as treasurer.) He spoke of numerous achievements by African Americans, always mindful of the distance most had traveled to reach any level of accomplishment. Perhaps one of the high points of the speech was when he boasted: "Even in America, the Negro brought in as a slave was not introduced into the economic life of the country as a competitor to the white man, but as an aid. I doubt whether any statesmen of the periods in which Negroes were brought to America as slaves would have continued the experiment if they had known that 1865 would have recorded Negroes to the number of four million on American soil, eventually to become economic competitors of white men."[38]

Such speeches propelled Jones at the pinnacle of his professional power. By this point in his career, he had a clearly articulated mission. Between 1915 and 1930, social workers, black and white, strove to construct a distinct professional identity, and Jones had a direct impact upon the development of this identity for all of social work. He was the first African American to be elected to the NCSW's Executive Board. One of the organization's objectives was to "define and secure professional standards for social work."[39] Throughout the 1920s, academic-training institutions became more prominent in the evolution of social work as a profession. In 1915, when Abraham Flexner, a representative of the Carnegie Foundation, declared that social workers were not professionals, there were only five professional social-work schools; by 1930 there were forty.[40]

During Jones's stint on the Executive Board (1926–33), he addressed and interpreted the social and economic concerns of the black community to a national and integrated audience. He eventually was elected vice president of the NCSW.[41] This platform enabled Jones to espouse the concerns of black social and economic welfare, and he was often able to place those concerns on the national agenda of social-work activity. For example, Jones continuously raised the issues of health, economics, and housing as it affected the African American population.

Social work was the only profession at the time that accepted blacks and whites equally into professional organizations. Though it is unclear how often these organizations were in fact racially integrated, many black social workers embraced the white social-work establishment. Jones and other black social workers were active in the AASW. The Social Work Club, which was founded in 1915 for black social workers, appears to have been abandoned by 1921. Jones insisted in 1928 that "[t]here is probably no profession in which Negro members are on as cordial relationships with white members as is that of the social worker."[42]

More established professions, such as medicine, nursing, science, law, and history, practiced segregation and/or discrimination within their professional memberships in the early twentieth century,[43] so African American professionals created their own governing organizations, including the National Medical Association in 1895, the National Bar Association in 1925,[44] and the National Association of Colored Graduate Nurses in 1908.[45] The NCSW was unique during this period in that it made no discrimination in the rank and file of its black and white members. Black social workers served on the Executive Board, division committees, and as division program speakers that addressed general programs of the conference. Though the NCSW did not officially discriminate, social workers encountered racist attitudes and Jim Crow policies in the institutions they served. Black social workers worked with Jim Crow institutions such as the settlement houses that were established by the 1920s to serve only black people. Whites directed many of these facilities. When white social workers served the black migrant population, they implemented Jim Crow guidelines in these institutions. Often white settlement houses created separate agendas for black and white newcomers. By and large, white settlement houses were not open to African Americans.[46]

This was of grave concern for many black social workers. Jones addressed these concerns through the national forum. His reception into the overall social-work profession had gone over well by the mid-1920s, and he now began to address the shortcomings of social work for black people on several other fronts. Jones wrote to an associate in Boston in 1926, "In our great America, relations between the various elements making up our population—native Protestants, Catholics, Jews, foreigners, Negroes, Indians—need constantly to be watched, that no disturbing propaganda may work havoc to the improving conditions."[47] Jones remained optimistic about the plight of the African American population.

It might appear that all was well with Jones and his concerns for black social welfare, but this was not the case. Other issues confronted the cadre of approximately five hundred specially trained black social workers on the eve of the Great Depression in 1928.[48] The number of trained black social workers reflected the efforts of several northern white social-service training schools and Jones's efforts with the fellowship programs that were offered through the

NUL. In spite of this major development, there were other issues to overcome. Behind the facade of inclusivity, Jones had to confront racial tensions.

In the South, only two schools had been established for black social workers by the 1920s: the Atlanta School of Social Work and Bishop Tuttle Training School for Social Workers of St. Augustine College in Raleigh, North Carolina. The Atlanta program, established in 1920, offered a general social-work approach. The Bishop Tuttle School of Social Work opened in 1925 and specialized in the training of social workers in conjunction with religious education.[49] Despite massive efforts to train black social workers, the results did not meet the growing demands of a burgeoning black urban population in the North and South.

Jones's untiring efforts to generate financial support for the NUL and its programs did not always meet with success. On numerous occasions, his efforts were not welcomed. Jones's proposals met with particular resentment in many parts of the South. Jones was rebuffed in cities such as Savannah and Augusta, Georgia; Charleston, South Carolina; Louisville, Kentucky; Richmond, Virginia; Charlotte, North Carolina; and Jacksonville, Florida. Jones stated: "[In the South,] in many instances, the proposals I made for Negro welfare had not been considered seriously for whites. The excuse given for rejecting proposals was frequently frankly stated: 'We are not doing that for white people. Surely you would not expect us to discuss such an undertaking for Negroes.'"[50]

Not only were Jones's efforts met with rejection from the white South, his attempts were sometimes perceived as "erroneous" from some members of the black community. Jones stated near the end of his career in 1940, "I often was met with rebuffs from prominent Negroes in the communities where we wished to establish Urban League branches for Negroes. Especially was this true in northern communities where the Negro leadership was based upon fights against segregation. Any social welfare effort in the interest of Negroes was immediately branded as an attempt to segregate them."[51] Migration had already complicated relations between "home people" and "old settlers" in many cities. Scholarship on black urban migration reveals that the growing tensions between the two groups were not unique to any city in particular; each had a unique situation. For instance, the historian Peter Gottlieb reveals that in Pittsburgh, "tensions that arose from growing differences of class and culture within the African-American population were not overcome by the rising awareness of a common racial identity."[52] The historian James R. Grossman states that "Chicago's black middle-class residents assumed that the migrants had to be guided and controlled from the moment they stepped from the train. . . . By inculcating restraint, the Old Settlers hoped to protect the migrants' souls and pocketbooks, while preserving the community's honor."[53] Chicago's established black middle class often resented the idea of segregation—which grew more apparent with the arrival of southern black migrants. The historian Kenneth Kusmer discovered that the NUL's efforts in Cleveland in the early twentieth century were also slow to gain acceptance in the black community. The Urban League was likened to the Negro Welfare Association in Cleveland, "limited in its effectiveness by the theory of social work then in vogue." The Urban League and the Negro Welfare Association were similar to white welfare organizations such as the Charity Organization Society. They were viewed as having "fostered the view that poverty and economic dislocation resulted, in many instances, from the failure of the lower class to adopt bourgeois goals and standards."[54]

Some urban communities in the South were not open to Jones and the work of the NUL. In 1925, the Neighborhood Union of Atlanta refused to become affiliated with the Urban League. The Neighborhood Union had done an enormous job of aiding the downtrodden black community of Atlanta since its inception in 1908, largely through its alignment with the Community Chest in Atlanta. Black women had worked hard to establish "free kinder-gartens, day nurseries, and orphanages" in addition to the union's day-to-day operations. The NUL wanted to use the organization as a model and requested that its records be turned over to NUL headquarters in New York. Atlanta's established black-community caretakers were not willing to cooperate with Jones and the NUL in this joint venture.[55] Lugenia Burns Hope, nationally recognized as a black southern reformer and the wife of Atlanta University's president John Hope, led the battle against the efforts of the NUL. "She made it clear . . . that the union would neither merge with the league nor totally turn over its community work in Atlanta to the league."[56] Though Jones's motives were benign, the dispute with the Neighborhood Union reveals a level of arrogance and superiority that may have accompanied the NUL. Atlanta was a prime example of the strife that Jones confronted in the urban South.

Jones and the NUL confronted a different set of issues in Detroit, the city in which the NUL encountered the most difficulty. Detroit was divided along ethnic lines long before the NUL sought to establish itself there. Black Americans had begun to migrate to Detroit during the Civil War and immediately after in search of educational opportunities. By the late nineteenth century, a small group of southern black businessmen and professionals had settled there.[57] Other northern cities experienced similar settlement patterns, but Detroit remained the most challenging city for the national office of the Urban League, before and immediately after World War I. "The pressing needs of both industry and migrants transformed Detroit into a social laboratory demonstrating the role of the Urban League in aiding southern migrants' adjustment to urban-industrial life."[58] This was largely due to the fact that by then the automobile industry was its main employer.

The Detroit branch of the Urban League was established in 1916, and John C. Dancy Jr. became its "conservative spokesman" in 1918.[59] Prior to Dancy, Forrester B. Washington was the executive secretary, during which time he became a "prominent national authority on black urban problems." The Detroit Urban League was the main supplier of black workers for Chrysler, Dodge, Studebaker, Briggs, and Cadillac.[60] Washington remained a strong advocate of black economic empowerment through jobs in the industries of Detroit. However, it was Dancy who established the long-term relationships with the auto industry during the First World War.

Dancy's relationship with the automobile tycoons was cemented over the next two decades. In the 1920s, "industrialization created the dependency relationship between key black leaders and Henry Ford."[61] A host of black ministers and business owners aligned themselves with Ford and the industrial establishment.[62] By the 1930s, growing dissent over the labor movement had become a major source of friction between the Urban League's Detroit and national offices. By this time, the NUL had "endorsed collective bargaining and also the CIO."[63] Detroit's black industrial workers were trapped between the growing union movement among white autoworkers and the often violent hostility of the companies.

The issue of unionism was larger than what was going on within the NUL. African Americans had been a major concern in the labor movement from as early as the 1870s as a result of the founding of the Knights of Labor in 1869.[64] As the growing concerns of American industrialization and world-market imperialism became more entrenched in the American workplace, so did the concerns of Jones and the NUL with securing permanent employment for black Americans. On the eve of the Depression in May 1929, *Opportunity* reported "no real advance in the attitude of organized labor toward the colored workers and [that] sentiment in labor circles is still set against Negro participation."[65]

Black America's hostility to some unions and unionization in general was nothing new. Black workers were usually used as strikebreakers. They commonly did not trust unions and had not been allowed to participate in collective bargaining. Often black workers were dismissed once agreements were reached and white union strikers returned to work. By the time of the Great Depression, 1929 to 1941, black workers were even further displaced.

Jones was a prominent expert on the economic conditions of the African American community as early as the mid-1920s. Government officials and practically every known sociologist and economist sought his advice. Karl F. Phillips, the Commissioner of Conciliations in the U.S. Department of Labor, communicated regularly with Jones and sought his recommendation for nearly every African American applicant that came before him seeking federal employment.[66] Jones obliged him with the necessary information or referred him to more appropriate individuals. No doubt, this contact assisted Jones in being appointed the Advisor of Negro Affairs in the Department of Commerce from 1933 to 1936.

Jones accomplished an enormous amount through his work with the NUL and his active role with the NCSW during the 1920s. He was a national figure by the eve of the Great Depression. He aligned himself with other leading black and white intellectuals as an outspoken social reformer; no other African American social economist played such a role. The 1930s saw Jones's political, social, and cultural profile rise even further. In addition to his talents in economics, Jones became a leading national spokesman in the quest for justice in black America.

4. Between New York and Washington

Although I have no idea as to where to turn for support, the need is so urgent that I shall not be satisfied until I have exhausted every possible effort to assure to the Negro population that their cause is adequately and forcefully represented in Washington by those to whom they look for action.
—Eugene Kinckle Jones, August 4, 1933

The late 1920s ushered in a new day in national reform policies, and Eugene Kinckle Jones had proven himself as a progressive reformer. This chapter will closely examine his fund-raising activities, his relations with white philanthropists, and his position within the Department of Commerce during the New Deal.

From 1900 through the 1970s, four American presidential administrations have been labeled as progressive: those of Theodore Roosevelt, Woodrow Wilson, Franklin D. Roosevelt, and Lyndon B. Johnson.[1] Jones had political ties to the two presidents in office during his tenure with the NUL, Woodrow Wilson and Franklin D. Roosevelt, whose administrations sought and received advice and active participation from Jones and the NUL. Jones advised the Wilson administration in its efforts to establish the Division of Negro Economics in April 1918. Though the position was short-lived, he supported the appointment of George Edmund Haynes as the director of the division. In February 1918, Jones and a group of four leading black and white citizens urged the Department of Labor "to appoint one or two blacks in each of its bureaus concerned with the adjustment and distribution of Negro labor."[2] This act is what eventually led to Haynes's appointment.

Some black community leaders supported instead the appointment of Giles Jackson, a successful lawyer from Richmond, Virginia. "He was the first black attorney to be admitted to practice before the Supreme Court of Appeals in Virginia (November 30, 1887) without benefit of a Yale law degree or Howard University degree."[3] W. E. B. DuBois wrote to Jones in April 1918 inquiring about Jackson, "[H]ow can I get at the facts of his career?"[4] While informing

DuBois of how he could "best expose" Jackson, Jones took the opportunity to inform DuBois of Dr. George E. Haynes's acceptance of the "position of labor adviser to Secretary of Labor."[5] Jones remained an invaluable resource for the federal government through the Department of Commerce over the next three decades.

By the eve of the Depression, the NUL was finding it even harder to keep up financially with its operations. A climate of economic scarcity had settled in many quarters of the philanthropic world before the onslaught of the Depression, but Jones was determined that the work of the NUL would not be terminated. Many philanthropists, such as Julius Rosenwald, were swamped with requests to help support every imaginable cause. Jones personally solicited Rosenwald's financial support for the NUL; the two had developed a friendly relationship over the years. The economic concerns of the nation and particularly those of African American workers were mounting long before the stock-market crash.

In March 1929, Jones was informed by E. C. Scott, the secretary to Rosenwald, that "the Julius Rosenwald Fund is now handling appropriations to national organizations." He further stated to Jones, "[Y]our appeal should be made to the Fund rather than to him."[6] On April 4, 1929, Edwin R. Embree, the president of the Julius Rosenwald Fund, wrote to Jones expressing doubt as to the fund's continual financial support of the NUL. While Embree expressed interest in the work of the Urban League, he cautioned Jones not to expect the Rosenwald Fund's usual level of support. He informed Jones that the fund was "anxious to keep at a minimum our contributions to general national agencies and wish[ed] to keep on the list only those that are doing very concrete pieces of work that cannot be cared for otherwise."[7] This represented the first time the Urban League was questioned about whether it implemented a national agenda. Perhaps Rosenwald's representatives had an even greater concern; they questioned whether the African American cause was in fact a national one.

As was typical of Jones's approach to the work of the Urban League, this was not about to deter his efforts. He immediately responded to Embree that his letter was "somewhat disappointing" and began to address the fund's concerns. Jones mapped out for Embree the main points of the Urban League's work as follows:

1. To ascertain by careful inquiry the social needs of Negroes in cities;
2. To try to have these needs met if possible by existing agencies, and if not, through its own endeavors;
3. To provide for the training of Negro social workers who may attack these problems constructively either through the Urban League itself

or through agencies that have already undertaken social programs for Negroes or may be induced to do so;

4. To work towards enlarging the industrial opportunities of Negroes by removing objections to employing them by whatever means of persuasion that may be possible.[8]

Jones sought to assure Embree that "the League is the only organization of its kind working in interest of the Negro."[9] After describing the Urban League's operations in great detail, Jones developed the ultimate appeal. He wrote to Embree that he had received word from Ruth Standish Baldwin, "who was the real founder of the Urban League movement."[10] Baldwin had written to Jones expressing her admiration for the NUL's work, and he provided Embree with what he referred to as her "unsolicited" commentary: "You cannot, however, overestimate my interest in the work of the League, nor my gratification at the way in which its usefulness has grown and developed, nor yet my hopes for its future."[11] Jones believed that Baldwin's words were of the greatest usefulness in this time of need. Veiled in slight sarcasm, Jones stated to Embree that he was forwarding this particular letter "in view of suggestions from some quarters that possibly the League's program was not quite definite enough."[12] He opined, "[I]t is interesting to know just what Mrs. Baldwin thinks now of the work after nearly nineteen years of the organization's activities."[13] The economic scarcity of the period was not about to defeat Jones's mission of securing funding for the NUL.

By the time of the Great Depression in 1929, Jones and the NUL had become important factors in addressing the social and economic woes that confronted black America. Jones's experiences during his first two decades at the NUL prepared him for the Depression. By the time "the most catastrophic period in American history had consumed the nation with economic dislocation,"[14] Jones was in a position to offer sound advice about the African American condition. In April 1929, President Herbert Hoover wrote to Jones concerning the economic condition of the African American population. He stressed to Jones that "the first step toward being a good citizen is to achieve economic independence." President Hoover further pointed out that "the work of the National Urban League to train Negroes in the city to find new lines of occupation is fundamental to the progress of the race."[15] It is likely that Jones initiated this communication with Hoover, as he traditionally shared the concerns of the NUL with every president in office during his tenure.

As the stock-market crash consumed the nation's attention, the efforts of Eugene Kinckle Jones and other trained black social workers intensified. Jones and the NUL had succeeded in developing a cadre of individuals to deal with the dispossessed black urban population. Jones had not only worked to secure avenues to train black social workers but had fought to have them accepted as professionals of equal status to white social workers. Much of the racial duality in American social work during the early twentieth century was based upon the separate but unequal principles of Jim Crow.[16]

Jones had already begun to address the financial concerns of the overworked NUL by the end of the 1920s. Other issues were mounting around the nation for black Americans, particularly the concerns of labor and employment. The labor issue did not suddenly appear in black America as a result of the Great Depression; black Americans were dealing with the lack of employment opportunities long before the national concerns triggered by the stock-market crash.[17] The NUL had dealt with the labor issue since its founding in 1910. However, it was Jones's "leadership and character [that] shaped [the] NUL during those crucial years."[18] A host of field workers, social workers, and local affiliate executives and organizers aided this national cause. Jones worked constantly to establish as many local branches of the NUL as possible.

In 1914, Jones decided to bring on an assistant to aid him in the national office. He hired T. Arnold Hill, a native of Richmond and a graduate of Virginia Union University who had completed one year of study in economics and sociology at New York University. By December 1916, the national office had decided that Hill would best serve the Chicago community by establishing a local affiliate there. Hill headed the Chicago branch of the Urban League until he was summoned back to New York in 1925 to serve as the director of the newly established Department of Industrial Relations. This division of the NUL worked directly with industry to help secure employment for black urban populations. It aimed "to standardize and coordinate the local employment agencies of the League to assure applicants for work an efficient and helpful service and employers efficient workers."[19] Hill became the linchpin for this important component of the NUL's agenda.[20] Between 1914 and 1925, Hill worked diligently to convince the city of Chicago of the urgency to include African Americans for industrial employment. Following the race riots of 1919, Hill and other black and white leaders in Chicago worked hard to provide the black community with "proper police protection."[21] The historian William M. Tuttle noted that "while the lynchings of the Red Summer were usually confined to the South, practically half of the epidemic of race riots burst forth in Northern and border states."[22]

In the meantime, Jones was still working to secure financial support for the day-to-day operations of the NUL. He remained tenacious in his solicitation of funds. As the 1920s drew to a close, the NUL faced greater financial difficulty.

Jones kept among the files of the NUL a statement entitled "The Octopus and Its Tentacles," which detailed the endowed foundations that were allegedly "destroying faith in God and in a duly constituted and orderly government." The seven foundations chronicled were the Rosenwald Foundation, the Laura Spelman Rockfeller Foundation, the General Education Board, the Carnegie Corporation, the Milbank Memorial Fund, the Common/Wealth Fund, and the Russell Sage Foundation. The document stated that the seven had a combined endowment fund of about five hundred million dollars. They "were bound together each of the seven to do its particular work, but welded together for the destruction of civilization and regular and orderly government."[23] The Rosenwald Fund was not believed to be one of the seven, "but nevertheless is working with them for the same purpose."[24]

It is not clear whether Jones gave the document much attention. He wrote to the Julius Rosenwald Fund on January 2, 1930, to thank it for its continual support of the NUL's programs. While wishing the officers of the fund a prosperous New Year, he made it clear that "we are hoping that we may continue to merit your confidence."[25] From the time of its founding, the NUL did not typically participate in direct-action agitation as did organizations such as the NAACP. Most of the NUL's budget came from the Altman, Carnegie, Rosenwald, and Rockefeller philanthropies, and therefore it "placed its stock in conciliation and private negotiations."[26] The NUL did not generally advocate political agitation, but this would change by the late 1920s.

In 1928, Elmer Carter succeeded Charles S. Johnson as the editor of *Opportunity*, and the journal's focus switched to highlighting economics and politics, with a growing emphasis on economics in the African American community and the lack of political access. Conditions for blacks in the American labor force had not improved, and the AFL in 1927 still refused to accept African Americans.[27] While T. Arnold Hill of the Industrial Relations Division of the NUL continued to deal with the labor issue, Jones kept the national office focused on the Urban League's financial security.

As the NUL prepared to celebrate its twentieth anniversary in 1930, Jones appeared more concerned with the development of the league's national agenda. He wrote again to the Rosenwald Fund on January 22, 1930, soliciting "an appropriation of $10,000."[28] He had "three distinct requests for the year 1930." First, he sought the renewal of the fund's annual contribution of one thousand dollars. The second and third requests were "associated one with the other." Jones made a rather substantial request for ten thousand dollars to cover the cost of salaries, office assistance, and traveling expenses for field secretaries at new branches. He further sought a sum not to exceed fifty thousand dollars to be available over a period of two years to enable the Urban League to begin working in communities where there were no league activities.[29] Extant records do not reveal the results of this request. The Rosenwald Fund likely was not able to accommodate it, however, particularly in the midst of the Depression.

The Rosenwald Fund appears to have cut its existing funding to the NUL as well. On July 2, 1931, Jones wrote to the fund's representative, George R. Arthur, expressing disappointment that a "Mr. Squires was not included" as a fellowship appointee.[30] Jones had assumed that the fund would support three appointments. Arthur responded a week later, telling Jones, "I know that you are disappointed concerning Mr. Squires," and seeking to assure him that "the Committee did not see its way clear to grant more than two fellowships to your organization this year." He closed by informing Jones that the number of "fellowship grants this year was not as many as those granted for the 1930–1931 period."[31] In October 1931, Jones wrote to Edwin R. Embree of the Rosenwald Fund to thank him for an autographed copy of his new book, *Brown America*. He assured Embree that he would review it for the upcoming issue of *Opportunity* and enclosed a "personal" copy of the Urban League's most recent annual report. In closing, he stated to Embree, "I hope that you can peruse [the report] so that you can gain a clearer idea of the reason I consider the Urban League's program most important and far-reaching."[32]

Jones's address to the annual meeting of the National Urban League in 1932 made national headlines. As the *New York Times* headline proclaimed, "Executive of Urban League Reports 'Almost Criminal' Discrimination on Jobs." Jones stated that "Negro unemployment had been subjected to almost criminal discrimination in the current depression."[33] The Depression hit black America hard, and Jones and the NUL carefully monitored every sign of worsening conditions. Jones's commitment to the NUL and its national agenda was intense, but his role in the NUL had not yet reached its zenith.

By 1932, Jones had shifted his attention toward joining with the efforts of the New Deal and what relief could be secured for distressed black urban communities. Jones appears to have been overworked by this time in his career. In conjunction with the NUL, he remained a major force on the Executive Board of the NCSW from 1925 to 1933. After his stint with the Executive Board, Jones prepared to begin spending part of his time in Washington as a New Deal agent.

In April 1933, Jones submitted to President Franklin D. Roosevelt a forty-five-page report summarizing the "important social facts pertaining to the Negro population of the United States." Jones declared, "[T]oo often when steps are taken to ameliorate social conditions Negroes are not given equitable consideration."[34] Jones concluded with an excellent summation the African American condition in several categories: population, occupational status, unemployment and relief, special problems of employment, education, health, housing, recreation and leisure, delinquency, and civil rights.[35]

Jones continued to solicit the Julius Rosenwald Fund to assist with the work of the Industrial Relations Department of the NUL. In an effort to continue to monitor New Deal regulations and agencies, in July 1933 he wrote again to Edwin R. Embree, the president of the fund. The NUL wished to establish a temporary office to facilitate "the hearings on the codes for the various industries and to have a central point there where we can receive complaints from various communities of the failure of Negroes to receive fair consideration."[36] Jones felt that this would keep T. Arnold Hill better informed in the New York office of the NUL.

On August 1, 1933, Jones learned that Embree did not turn down the proposal out of hand, but he did suggest a rather surprising merger: "I have long hoped that some merger or union could be effected between the two Negro national agencies whose headquarters are New York—the Urban League and the NAACP."[37] He further wrote, "[F]riends and potential givers have no single agency through which they can express their interest."[38] The fund believed that the two organizations could be most useful if they formed a unified front. The fund was concerned about the decrease in financial support during the Depression years. Embree closed his letter with a further surprise: "So important does this matter seem to us in this office that we feel unwilling to make further contributions to either of these organizations in their present state of division."[39]

Jones's response was swift and direct: "[T]he programs of the two organizations have been so different in their approach and methods that no action has been taken looking towards the consummation of the idea."[40] Jones did express a guarded willingness to consider the proposal: "Knowing as you do the purposes and programs of the two organizations and the differences in their respective approaches to problems we face, . . . I would be much interested in hearing from you as to the means you would propose for effecting the merger."[41] But he remained skeptical about the proposed merger, and his attention was growing more attuned to what was happening in Washington, D.C., to relieve the suffering of black people through the aid of the federal government.

During Jones's time in Washington and away from the NUL, he guarded the national office with a watchful eye. Though cautious, he endeavored to make the NUL's presence felt during his tenure in Washington. Jones repeatedly advocated the philosophy of the NUL through his internal access within the government. As Guichard Parris and Lester Brooks conclude, "Kinckle Jones's major contribution during this time was in representing black interests at the inner core of the federal establishment."[42] Perhaps no other individual amplified nationwide black unemployment and the need for economic stability to the extent that Jones did through his direct involvement with the federal government from 1933 through 1936.

On October 18, 1933, the *New York Times* announced, "Roper Appoints E. K. Jones, Negro Economist, to Head Racial Problems Study Board."[43] Jones's appointment was a major milestone within the Department of Commerce. He was to "head the Commerce Department unit for the study of Negro problems."[44] In October 1933, Jones took a temporary leave of absence from his position as executive secretary of the NUL to direct this new division of the Commerce Department from 1933 to1936. T. Arnold Hill served as the acting executive secretary during his leave.[45]

The *New York Times* proclaimed Jones "an institution in himself."[46] In spite of the enormous praise he received, Jones's appointment with the Department of Commerce as Advisor on Negro Affairs did not meet with unanimous support in the black community. Carter G. Woodson criticized Jones and other black leaders who endorsed the Roosevelt ticket for president in 1932. "Woodson condemned blacks who were appointed to 'Jim Crow' federal positions set aside to reward Negro politicians."[47] Woodson was adamant in his stance against those who expressed any admiration for the American political system. While most blacks had joined "Roosevelt's bandwagon by 1936, Woodson refused, contending that 'the Negro should not cast his vote for a party that does not recognize him.'"[48] He went so far as to condemn Mary McLeod Bethune, who headed Roosevelt's Special Advisory Committee. He admonished everyone who worked under her guidance, known as the Black Cabinet. Bethune was also the national president of the organization that Woodson founded, the Association for the Study of Negro Life and History, from 1935 to 1950.[49]

Jones was engaged in the activities of the Roosevelt administration from the start, as an important member the Black Cabinet. Shortly after Jones's arrival in Washington, he began receiving correspondence from Jesse O. Thomas, the southern field director of the NUL. Thomas informed Jones on December 16, 1933, that "the grossest kind of discrimination is practiced against Negroes in Jackson."[50] Thomas quoted a man from Jackson, Mississippi, who "claimed that he and two hundred other Negroes were working under the CWA [Civil Works Administration] and receiving only thirty cents an hour when their cards were marked forty cents."[51] The situation in Jackson illustrates what a major task Jones and others like him were charged with. Despite the New Deal's national efforts, its distribution had to be monitored against local acts of racial discrimination. It was found that much improvement was needed in the local employment situation for African Americans in Jackson. Thomas informed Jones: "On the million dollar post office, the only Negro labor employed was unskilled labor. Some of the work included in the CWA project is the repairing of school buildings. They are using white mechanics to repair Negro school buildings when there are any number of Negro mechanics in Jackson who are competent and have been on relief."[52] This was the kind of activity that Jones was referring to in April 1933 when he urged Frances Perkins, the Secretary of Labor, not to overlook the concerns of black labor. "In a widely-publicized letter in April, Perkins assured . . . Eugene Kinckle Jones, that blacks would not be overlooked in the administration's vast reconstruction plans . . . for employment and relief."[53] It seems that even Perkins could not have predicted the outcome of the events in Jackson.

As the historian Clarke Chambers has noted, "[O]f all Franklin Roosevelt's official family, none perhaps had greater influence on the shaping of domestic policies than the spirited and pragmatic Frances Perkins."[54] A social worker by profession, she had also advised Roosevelt when he was governor of New York. Therefore, it was no surprise when she was appointed Secretary of Labor in late 1932.[55] Perkins belonged to the "women's network" in Washington during the New Deal, a group of middle-class white women who were involved in the early twentieth-century suffrage movement. Many among the women's network were close friends of Eleanor Roosevelt. The historian Susan Ware found that "the network encompassed virtually all of the women in top federal jobs in Washington in the 1930s."[56] Ware further states that "the only omission was prominent black educator Mary McLeod Bethune, head of the Office of Minority Affairs in the National Youth Administration from 1936 to 1944."[57] Though Ware suggests that Bethune probably saw herself as the representative of black people, it is without question that the women's network did not include her in its social gatherings due to her race. It was during their many social outings that these women were able to strategize. Ware concluded that the network was based upon "close friendship and loyalty"; ultimately, it was "both a sad and provocative commentary on the 1930s and the attitudes the other women brought to their government jobs."[58]

Not to be deterred by the obviously racist attitudes of the era, Bethune, Jones, and a host of other Black Cabinet advisors gathered in Washington in late 1933. According to the historian Harvard Sitkoff, "[T]he Roosevelt administration perpetuated more of the discrimination and segregation inherited from previous decades than it ended."[59] In spite of the obvious day-to-day persistence of racist attitudes, the "New Deal's arousal of sympathy for the forgotten man generated reform impulses that would revolutionize the black freedom struggle."[60] This period would later be labeled the Second Reconstruction by some scholars.[61]

Initially, Roosevelt had no intention of establishing a position that would allow anyone to oversee the African American interest in the recovery program. His greatest fear was that he would face a backlash from influential southern Democrats. Will Alexander and Edwin Embree approached the president with the idea for a new position within the Department of Commerce in early 1933. The president did not approve of the position until the Rosenwald Fund agreed to pay the salary for a special assistant to work on the economic status of African Americans; he was then free to bypass congressional approval.

Ironically, the usually liberal Secretary of the Interior Harold Ickes appointed the southern, young, white, religiously oriented Clark Foreman. The black press admonished the appointment of a white southerner to address the needs and concerns of black America.[62] Black community leaders were appalled in spite of Foreman's liberal background. Aubrey Williams and Foreman were two noted southern reformers who helped to "shape and administer, respectively, the Works Progress Administration and Public Works Administration";[63] they included nondiscriminatory approaches in their programs. After much resistance from black leaders over the selection of Foreman, the Rosenwald Fund decided to finance a black secretary as well. Robert Weaver was picked to fill this position.[64] Weaver was a recent graduate of Harvard University with a doctorate in economics, and his appointment met with approval from African American leadership.[65] In spite of this major effort to move forward, prior to 1934 Ickes and his assistants accomplished "little as watchdogs for the Negro's welfare."[66]

By early 1934, Ickes had obtained the president's approval to form an interdepartmental committee on Negro affairs. Eugene Kinckle Jones of the Commerce Department, Robert L. Vann of the Justice Department, Forrester B. Washington of the Federal Emergency Relief Administration (FERA), and Harry Hunt of the Farm Credit Administration, along with Ickes, Foreman, and Weaver, began meeting with white representatives of the National Recovery Administration (NRA), the Civilian Conservation Corporation (CCC), the Agriculture Department, and the military services. By 1935, several young black men had been granted positions in some of cabinet departments and New Deal agencies. Despite regular meetings, the committee would claim few victories during Roosevelt's first term. Jones and William Pickens of the NAACP, however, were "seasoned veterans for the civil rights movement."[67] They helped lay the groundwork for the modern civil-rights movement.

The historian Patricia Sullivan contends that "the New Deal era marked a departure from the national complacency that characterized the 1920s. For those who had not participated in the prosperity of the previous decade, it was a welcome change."[68] Jones and those involved with the interdepartmental work viewed the 1930s as a great opportunity for overall advancement in the African American community.

This interdepartmental group held its first meeting on the morning of February 7, 1934, in the Department of the Interior. The meeting was chaired and called to order by Clark Foreman, the Advisor on Economic Status of Negroes. This group was formed as a result of the "heads of the Departments and Administrations [having been] asked to designate someone as responsible for the participation of the Negroes in the work of each department."[69] According to the minutes, the first meeting "showed a large attendance."[70] Several prominent individuals were a part of the group that began doing the important work of securing for the African American population its share of government relief. Along with Jones from the Department of Commerce, the following individuals were present:

E. H. Shinn, Department of Agriculture
Phil Campbell, AAA (Agriculture Adjustment Administration)
Robert L. Vann, attorney general's office
Forrester B. Washington, CWA
J. J. McEntee, Emergency Conservation Work
H. A. Hunt, Farm Credit Administration
Edward F. McGrady, Department of Labor
Charles F. Roos, NRA
William D. Bergman, Navy
G. R. Clapp, Tennessee Valley Authority
W. H. McReynolds, Treasury Department
W. D. Searle, War Department
Clark Foreman, Interior Department
Robert C. Weaver, Interior Department.[71]

Each individual was introduced and asked to "tell in two or three minutes of the work of his department as it affected particularly the Negro population."[72] Jones stated that "his Division grew out of a conference of twelve Negroes called together by Secretary Roper to advise with him on the things the department of Commerce can do to improve the general economic conditions among Negroes, with special reference to business and business activities. Their idea has been that Negro business cannot qualify unless the Negro's consumer purchasing power is raised."[73] Jones's division was tasked with "putting new life in Negro business to avoid the unfortunate failure of the past."[74] This committee met periodically during Roosevelt's first term. Despite their efforts, their concerns and advice fell on deaf ears. The social-work scholar Jacob Fisher contends that, "With the exception of Ickes and Perkins, perhaps no one in high office in the government considered racial discrimination of major significance when compared with the greater objectives of business recovery, the end of mass unemployment, higher farm prices, banking reform, social security, and the other stated objectives of the New Deal."[75] Even Roosevelt refused to address the NAACP's demands for an antilynching bill in the 1930s.[76] Perhaps the greatest shortcoming of the Roosevelt administration was the omission of black representation on the Committee on Economic Security.

In the fall of 1934, the president appointed the Advisory Council to the Committee on Economic Security. Most of the council was made up of state and local politicians, along with several prominent social workers. Frank P. Graham chaired the committee, and Paul Kellogg, editor of *The Survey*, was vice chairman.[77] There were no black representatives on this committee, which helped to formulate one the most important legislative bills of the entire New Deal, Social Security. The council reported to the Senate Finance Committee, which went to the president for congressional approval.[78]

The NUL and NAACP made a joint effort to influence the Social Security Act from its inception. Walter White of the NAACP asked Sen. Robert F. Wagner of New York, who sponsored the bill, "whether it contained adequate safeguards against discrimination on account of race."[79] Although Wagner assured both organizations, it was to no avail. In the end, the Social Security program "excluded agricultural and domestic employees from its provisions for unemployment compensation and old-age insurance."[80] The NAACP argued that it dealt a "direct blow at Negro workers," while the NUL protested to Roosevelt that it "excluded 65 percent of the Negroes throughout the country."[81]

Rather than become consumed by obvious omissions, Jones directed his attention toward increasing black labor opportunities. Some scholars have concluded that the Black Cabinet had very little success.[82] On the surface, such a conclusion appears to be substantiated, particularly when the concerns of "Negro . . . unemployment and the need for low-cost housing"[83] are the measures by which scholars calculate success. The gains that African Americans did achieve during the New Deal were largely due to the relentless efforts of Jones and a cadre of black professionals who worked with Mary McLeod Bethune and the Roosevelt administration.

In June 1935, Jones reported to Secretary of Commerce Daniel C. Roper that he had delivered ninety-one public addresses since taking office in November 1933. In practically every appearance, Jones addressed the economic and social-welfare concerns of African Americans. He stated, "[A]t every available opportunity, in conferences and when addressing public gatherings, the services offered by the Department of Commerce through the Washington and District offices were presented."[84] Jones aided black employment by helping to create 294 white-collar jobs by 1935 in thirty selected cities and outlining "a plan for the study of Negro Business Resources" through "the President's work relief program."[85] Jones reported that "the main object of the study would be to procure data which can be utilized to improve general business practices among Negroes, and to expand their business institutions."[86] Jones took this message of economic empowerment to black communities in Washington, D.C.; Massillon, Ohio; New York City; Montreal; Quebec; Canton, Ohio; Dover, Delaware; and Flushing, New York, to name a few of the places he traveled. Chester H. McCall, the assistant to the secretary, informed Jones that Roper was pleased with his work for the quarter; "the most appropriate comment we can make is keep up the good work."[87]

Jones was the voice of the African American community in the Department of Commerce at this time. Roper reported in October 1935 that Jones "worked chiefly through the Bureau of Foreign and Domestic Commerce as liaison between the Bureau and Negro business men and students of economic questions to help Negro business and to increase the purchasing power of the members of the race."[88] While Jones served as the Advisor on Negro Affairs in the Department of Commerce, several studies of great importance to the black community were conducted and published. Jones reported in July 1936 that his office was continuing to "work on the four studies which have been in progress during the past year."[89] They were: Negro Air Pilots, Negro Chambers of Commerce, Negro Trade Associations, and Negro Insurance Company Failures.

Under Jones's auspices, the bureau also revised and distributed a "list of Negro chambers of Commerce" that was "distributed at strategic points."[90] In addition, Jones's office sent out information concerning the general economic status of African Americans. The mailing list was extensive: it included students, writers, interested citizens, advertising agencies, distributors, manufacturers, promoters, educational institutions, and public libraries. The information typically pertained to African American aviators, banks, chambers of commerce, insurance companies, manufacturers, newspapers and periodicals, retailers, and trade associations.[91] Jones and his contemporaries in Washington accomplished much on behalf of black Americans. To be sure, this was part of the early groundwork to the civil-rights movement. Jones and his colleagues informed the African American community of political and economic opportunities through the federal government. The historian Harvard Sitkoff claims that "a host of government publications and conferences made explicit the federal government's responsibility for issues of human rights."[92] This was the exact nature of Jones's work as part of the New Deal. Time and time again, he informed African Americans of assistance opportunities through the federal government's relief programs.

Jones worked nonstop during his tenure at the Department of Commerce. He reported in June 1936 that he had delivered 135 addresses all over the country between November 1, 1935, and June 30, 1936, pertaining to economic conditions in African American communities.[93] While in Washington, Jones did not neglect contacts with such noted black intellectuals as W. E. B. DuBois and the historian Rayford W. Logan. In the mid-1930s, DuBois prepared to launch his massive *Encyclopedia of the Negro*. Jones wrote to DuBois in October 1935, "I would be willing to cooperate in every possible way, especially in rendering service in the field in which I have had my largest experience."[94] Logan wrote to Jones in November 1936, "I am sure that Dr. DuBois will be grateful to you for suggestions that you may have to offer."[95] Jones assured Logan that he would probably have more suggestions as the project progressed. Whether in government or literature, Jones worked continuously to ensure a stake in American society for the African American population.

As Jones prepared to leave the Department of Commerce in December 1936, there were a total of 240 African Americans working throughout the department.[96] Secretary Roper later informed James A. Farley, the chairman of the Democratic National Committee, that "because of the well-organized condition in which Jones left his work, we have promoted Charles E. Hall, a Negro, who has been employed in the Census Bureau."[97] In 1936, Jones prepared to return full-time to his job as executive secretary of the NUL. Roper felt that Jones had rendered a valuable service "as Head of the Unit in the Bureau of Foreign and Domestic Commerce relating to Negro industrial relations."[98] Because of Jones's expertise in economics, this division of the government was poised to "render better and more effective service to the Negroes than theretofore."[99] Jones was a definite force to be reckoned with by the time of the Great Depression. He had proven himself effective regardless of whether he worked in government or as a social worker. He was a multi-talented figure who gained national attention.

5. Changing of the Guard

His character was as nearly perfect as a man's can be. He was
gentle, patient, and wise. His integrity was unshakable and was
equaled only by his courage. He understood the true nature of
American democracy, its weaknesses and its strength, its internal
group conflicts, and what needed to be done to fulfill its promises.
—Board of Trustees of the National Urban League
    on Eugene Kinckle Jones, 1954

As Jones returned to New York to resume his full-time position as
executive secretary of the NUL, a changing climate was emerging within the
social-work profession. Jones arrived in 1937 and began to engage directly
in providing social-work services for black people. Major changes within
the social-work profession, the NUL, and Jones's personal life loomed on
the horizon.

Many social workers were convinced by Roosevelt's second-term elec-
tion that New Deal policies would effectively address major social woes.
Particularly following the adoption of the Social Security Act in 1935, many
social reformers, black and white, began looking to government- rather than
community-initiated relief.[1] By the 1930s, there was a gradual move away
from the community settlement-house concept toward the establishment
of government welfare agencies. The 1920s model of casework as the para-
digm of social work lost center stage during the Depression. The social-work
scholar John H. Ehrenreich concludes that "with the advent of the Depression and its massive poverty, its newly energized social programs, its new
social work institutions, and its transformed relationship between social
workers and government, the twenties' model of professionalism became an
anachronism."[2] Ehrenreich further claims that "the rapid expansion of relief
programs following Roosevelt's inauguration as president had transformed
the relationship between relief and casework."[3] In short, social-work elites
could no longer claim that social work solely operated with respect to clients

and patrons. Furthermore, the profession was deeply split between the old guard and the rank-and-filers by the 1930s.

The best-known of the elite settlement-house social reformers, Jane Addams, died in 1935. According to the historian Judith Trolander, "[N]o one came along in the settlement movement to replace her in the public mind."[4] Even those settlement homes that remained by the mid-1930s began to realize that certain fundamental changes were necessary to keep up with the changing trends in social work. Perhaps the greatest failure of the settlement-house movement was that it did not embrace an overall integrated agenda during this time of Jim Crow segregation. The historian Elisabeth Lasch-Quinn concludes that race was the main cause of the movement's decline: "Not only did the settlements' failure to welcome black neighbors universally into their programs contribute to their long-term decline, but their restrictionism left the great promise of the movement unfulfilled."[5]

A group of social workers attempted to address racial injustice within the profession during the 1930s; this was often described as the "rank-and-file" movement among organized social work. Though the organization's greatest concern was the establishment of social-work unions, it played a major role in radical agitation during the 1930s. Most social workers identified the rank-and-file movement as the political left wing of social work. Social workers who belonged to the rank and file often focused their energy on securing avenues "for linking the broad social objectives of social work and the labor movement."[6] Perhaps the organization's greatest success was the establishment and inauguration of its journal, *Social Work Today,* in 1934, in which many of their concerns were addressed.[7] This journal and the rank and filers in general tended to be more radical in their outlook for social work. The journal was edited by the noted social-work scholar Jacob Fisher of the Bureau of Jewish Social Research and advised by major figures in social work such as Gordon Hamilton, Eduard C. Lindeman, Ira Reid, Roger Baldwin, and Mary Van Kleeck.[8] *Social Work Today* was the left-wing journal of the profession and a competitor with *The Survey,* which addressed more traditional and nonconfrontational issues of social work.[9] Jones was active in Washington at the organization's height. Though definitive evidence is lacking, it is unlikely that Jones affiliated with the group due to its radical dispositions.

Jacob Fisher, the chairman of the National Coordinating Committee of Social Service Employee Groups, was a dominant figure among the rank and filers. Fisher wrote in December 1936 to Edith Abbott, the president of the NCSW and a leading social-work figure at the University of Chicago, acknowledging her letter concerning "equal treatment of Negroes at the Indianapolis meeting"[10] of the NCSW in 1936, a major turning point for social relations among black and white social workers.

African American attendees of the 1936 meeting were not permitted into the hotel bar. Though African American members of the NCSW were lodging at the hotel and attending all the sessions of the conference, the hotel's racial codes did not permit them to socialize in the bar. Jacob Fisher and the members of the committee took this issue up with Abbott and the executives of the NCSW. Fisher questioned Abbott as to whether the act of discrimination violated the NCSW trade-union agreement. Rank and filers refused to let the incident go unchecked. Following the act of discrimination, the NCSW executive officers were never to allow the conference to be held in a place that did not accommodate black and white social workers equally. This was written into the bylaws of the conference because of the expressed concern of Fisher and other rank-and-file members.

Fisher began to correspond with Abbott concerning the Indianapolis incident. Abbott's response was ambiguous and reason enough for concern. Though change was evident in some white social workers, many were reluctant to deal with forced external change. Abbott responded to Fisher, "[M]y reason for thinking that we should take no action is that I believe that the business of the Conference is to make it possible for all of our membership to have an opportunity to attend all of our meetings and our official social gatherings."[11] Abbott did not agree that the conference should take up such issues as social gatherings; she further stated that "it would be a great mistake for the Conference to take any responsibility for providing opportunities of any kind in the local bars. . . . This is a matter which seems to many of us clearly outside the business of the Conference."[12] Abbott was adamant in her position, and she used several examples to illustrate her views on social matters outside the conference: "I do not think that it is the business of the Conference to assure any kind of recreational facilities to any of its members. If a golf club gives privileges to men and not to women, this seems to me a matter about which the Conference is not concerned. If a bar admits men and excludes women, this seems to me again a matter about which we have no concern. This applies also to the matter of any racial lines that may be drawn in these fields."[13]

The rank-and-file group did not drop the issue in the face of Abbott's opposition; they used every available avenue to denounce the actions of the hotel and the racial codes in the city of Indianapolis. Following the incident, the NCSW was cautious not to hold its meetings in locales with codes of racial discrimination. The National Coordinating Committee denounced the act of discrimination publicly in the organization's newsletter, *Trade Union*

Notes, on May 23, 1937. Perhaps to counteract Abbott's position, the editorial read that "the struggle for equal rights and opportunities for Negroes, for an anti-lynching law, and other such legislation requires the active support of all progressive social workers."[14] Abbott's indifference reveals a major lack of sensitivity about race relations within the social-work profession. Abbott and others like her controlled and determined the nature of many northern settlement houses. In most instances, their institutions did not address the plight of African Americans. This is made evident through their noncommittal attitudes and failures to address the total well-being of all people.

Aside from the overwhelming concerns of race in the settlement-house movement, other forces threatened peaceable relations within social work. During the 1937 meeting of the NCSW, the American Association of Schools of Social Work (AASSW) adopted the Master of Social Work degree as its qualification for professional social workers, to take effect in 1939.[15] This decision challenged the professional credentials of black social workers in the North and South. Atlanta University was the only school of social work in 1937 that offered an advanced degree for African Americans. Incidentally, the Supreme Court ruling in the 1938 *Gaines* decision impacted all professional training for African Americans for decades to come. White schools of social work were also about to be challenged on their existing notions of who could and would grant advance degrees. Social work began to find more allies at some historically black institutions of higher learning following the 1938 ruling.

The *Gaines* case initiated a groundswell of political and social unrest for the social-work profession. In the midst of internal changes sweeping through the profession, the Missouri Supreme Court handed down its famous decision in *Missouri ex rel. Gaines v. Canada* on December 12, 1938.[16] The decision led to numerous debates within programs of professional education for numerous southern states. North Carolina was the first state to challenge the existing status of graduate education offered black social workers as a result of the *Gaines* ruling.

Lloyd L. Gaines graduated in 1935 from the all-black Lincoln University in Jefferson City, Missouri, with honors. In 1936 he applied for admission to the University of Missouri Law School; his application was denied on the basis of his race. The Supreme Court ordered that if the University of Missouri did not admit Gaines, it must provide equal educational facilities and instruction at Lincoln University.[17]

Gaines sought legal counsel through the NAACP, which took this opportunity to "launch a campaign to desegregate Missouri's institutions of higher learning,"[18] which would challenge professional schools of training throughout the nation. Charles Hamilton Houston, the chief legal counsel of the NAACP, cautioned his "colleagues not to rush into court without adequate preparation."[19] He subsequently brought on Sidney Redmond, a black lawyer from St. Louis, who began to investigate inequalities between the University of Missouri and Lincoln University, which had no professional programs at the time. The historian Darlene Clark Hine has referred to these black lawyers who worked with Houston and the NAACP in the 1930s and 1940s as an "elite team."[20] The work of the NAACP lawyers would eventually prove successful.

The Supreme Court in 1938 ruled with a seven-to-two majority opinion favoring the plaintiff. The court "secured the precedents" that would be needed in other state and local cases that eventually culminated in the abandonment of the separate-but-equal Jim Crow laws.[21] The majority opinion reads as follows: "A state denies equal protection of the laws to a black student when it refuses him admission to its all-white law school, even though it volunteers to pay his tuition at any law school in an adjacent state. By providing a law school for whites but not for blacks the state has created a privilege for one race and denied it to another."[22]

Following the *Gaines* decision, Missouri attempted to evade the issues of discrimination in higher education. The state was not serious about providing a law school for blacks at Lincoln University equal to that at the University of Missouri in Columbia and was left with the now-infamous decision of trying to provide education for African Americans in nearby states with scholarships. Nonresident African Americans were permitted to study law in Kansas, Nebraska, Iowa, and Illinois.[23] The law professor Mark Tushnet argues that "[t]he white resident is afforded legal education within the State; the Negro resident having the same qualifications is refused it there and must go outside the State to obtain it. . . . [T]hat is a denial of the equality of legal right to the enjoyment of the privilege which the State has set up, and the provision for the payment of tuition fees in another State does not remove the discrimination."[24]

Eventually the *Gaines* decision ended in a law of agitation for white southern educational institutions; it questioned the social systems within all of the southern United States. Houston and the NAACP's team of lawyers had hoped that they would be able to argue in the *Gaines* case for equalization of facilities. Throughout the 1930s, Houston, the NAACP, and a small pool of civil-rights lawyers created social and racial unrest throughout the nation by deliberately and methodically arguing numerous court cases. Houston and his team of lawyers were hoping that *Gaines* would provide a far-reaching victory. Lloyd Gaines, by April 1939, could not be found for further court appearances, and the case was eventually dismissed. Despite its dismissal, by the late 1930s the case had established uneasiness throughout the nation, particularly the southern states that were not offering advanced education to its black citizens.[25] Though Gaines himself disappeared and the case could not be used to further argue for the equalization of facilities, it did establish a major precedent for future cases.

The writer Virginius Dabney noted that "southern educational systems . . . were on notice that they had to make far-reaching readjustments."[26] Most white educators agreed that separate educational facilities would best serve African American students. Following the NAACP's major victory with the *Gaines* case, "southern whites recognized the implicit challenge to the segregation system."[27] They were equally concerned that it would be too costly to establish two separate-but-equal schools for blacks and whites. Advocates of black social work in the South had hoped that the *Gaines* ruling would insist on enormous support to establish professional schools of social work at some predominately black colleges.

The historian Charles H. Wesley's study revealed that some southern states were laying the groundwork to establish graduate departments "as additions to the State colleges for Negroes."[28] Maryland, North Carolina, South Carolina, and Missouri made early strides to put such efforts into effect. African Americans who expressed great concern over the lack of opportunity for advanced education in the professions for black students, particularly in the South, skillfully orchestrated many of those early efforts.

Jones's work in the field of social work appears to have come full-circle by the late 1930s. His efforts to recruit black students to social work gained momentum following the *Gaines* decision. His argument found allies in historically black colleges in the South.

Jones remained conservative in all his work with the NUL, so it was no surprise when Dr. James E. Shepard of Durham, North Carolina, another noted conservative, took on the social-work establishment following the *Gaines* ruling. Shepard had waited to work within the realm of the law; the *Gaines* ruling had opened just such an opportunity for his conservative and conciliatory approach to race-related matters. Shepard courted the white Democratic establishment of North Carolina to financially support his institution, North Carolina College for Negroes (now North Carolina Central University; NCCU). Shepard was always methodical and behaved within the strictures of southern etiquette. He was considered the "principal spokesman of Negro conservatism" in North Carolina.[29] He did not support the NAACP's efforts to integrate the University of North Carolina at Chapel Hill (UNC) in 1933. Thomas Raymond Hocutt, a graduate of North Carolina College, applied to the school of pharmacy at UNC and was denied admission. When NAACP officials called on Shepard for assistance, he declined, believing that, "especially if stirred by out-of-staters, [the effort] would backfire and hurt the amicable status quo."[30] In keeping with his conservative approach, Shepard did not engage in the fight for African American advanced-education until the Missouri Supreme Court ruled in the *Gaines* case. Though Jones was not directly involved in North Carolina, Shepard's actions would have met with his approval. This was the kind of approach that Jones insisted upon for the development of black social work—nonconfrontational, but always seeking more opportunities to address the growing needs of urban black America.

As the founder and first president of North Carolina College for Negroes, Shepard led a struggle to establish an advanced degree in social work at NCCN following the *Gaines* ruling. The school was established at Durham, North Carolina, in 1910, and in 1925 became the first state-supported black liberal-arts college in the state. Due to a longtime affiliation with the Democratic governor Clyde R. Hoey, Shepard acquired generous amounts of money for the financial security of his institution.[31] Shepard had held an important position in the leadership of the black community in Durham for some time; by the 1930s, he was revered. The historian Walter Weare states, "[B]oth the sense of moral authority and the substance of community organization came . . . from the North Carolina Mutual and North Carolina College (North Carolina Central University)."[32]

Shepard worked to establish as many professional programs as possible at NCCU during his lifetime. In 1939, graduate work was begun in the liberal arts and professions. In 1940 and 1941, Shepard secured the establishment of the Schools of Law and Library Science, respectively.[33] Immediately after the *Gaines* decision, Shepard launched a campaign to create a social-work program at NCCU. At his death in 1947, a graduate program in social work had still not materialized.

On November 17, 1939, Shepard informed Marion Hathway, the executive secretary of the AASSW, that he desired "to make a formal application to the Executive Committee for the approval of a school of Social Work for Negroes at this Institution [NCCU]."[34] Shepard sought to assure Hathway that he had the support of "every social agency in the State" and was confident of the cooperation "of Duke University and the University of North Carolina in the establishment of such a department at this Institution."[35] Shepard stated that the need for the program was such that "the State already has both men and women in attendance at the Atlanta School of Social Work." He had already begun to seek state aid for the program and was certain it would "attract a reasonable number of students for the first year."[36] He made it clear that

NCCU would not act on the matter unless he received the absolute approval of her office.

Hathway balked at the establishment of a program at NCCU. She wrote in December 1939 to Roy M. Brown, the director of the Division of Public Welfare and Social Work at the University of North Carolina, concerning her recommendation. She stated that "part of the delay in sending this material is due to my reluctance to believe that the North Carolina program should not be encouraged."[37] Though her personal views were in agreement with Shepard, the committee appears to have viewed the situation with indifference. Therefore, Hathway's recommendations were ambiguous. Her concern, however, was a result of the *Gaines* decision. She wrote to Shepard in January 1940, "The establishment of a school of social work at the North Carolina College for Negroes raises a series of questions growing out of the *Gaines* decision."[38] Despite Hathway's plea for understanding, Shepard was unrelenting in his response. On January 23, 1940, he wrote: "I appreciate the frank way in which you have presented the matter, and your desire to be absolutely fair and considerate of all concerned. I must, however, state that I do not agree with some of your conclusions fully."[39] In closing, he asked that she forward the enclosed memorandum to "each member of the Executive Committee."[40]

Shepard's memorandum was entitled, "Effects of the Lloyd Gaines Decision in Programs of Professional Education in Certain States."[41] The memo addresses several issues raised by the committee's stated position. North Carolina and Missouri were the only two schools providing any state-supported professional training for African Americans. Shepard's memo forced Hathway and the committee to tackle the moral as well as the politically correct injunction. The moral question, according to Shepard, was as follows:

> Relative to making an exception in this case, it should be said that we as Negroes did not of our own volition create the separate school plan in the South. While we do not object to it, we feel that we are entitled as citizens to equal advantages and that the establishment of exceptional rules for us is generally another way of not assuming full responsibility for equal educational opportunities. We, therefore, feel that we are justified in objecting to any "back door entrance" into anything to which we are rightfully entitled.[42]

Shepard insisted upon the need for trained social workers in the black community. Further, although the "problem can be met by the maintenance of out-of-State scholarships . . . does the State, in making such arrangements, fulfill its obligations to provide Negroes with advantages afforded to white students?"[43]

Many black students, upon the completion of their studies at Atlanta's School of Social Work, were not returning to North Carolina. Therefore,

Shepard argued that the state could increase its pool of available social work-ers if a school were approved. He closed the memo by stating to Hathway that "[t]here are enough Negro colleges in the country to absorb every Negro college student in North Carolina. Does this fact suggest that there is no need for North Carolina to discharge its own obligation to its Negro citizens? In the final analysis, regardless of any statistical evidence which may be projected into the situation, the problem remains one of social justice."[44]

Brown wrote to Hathway in February: "[A]pparently what President Shepard is saying is that he wants the Association to find a way to approve the proposed curriculum in the North Carolina College for Negroes with-out declaring that such action is making an exception for his Institution."[45] Shortly thereafter, Hathway informed Shepard that the outgoing committee had received his memorandum and letter with great interest and concern.[46] The new Executive Committee did not meet until May. In the meantime, North Carolina was viewed as the major test case in social-work education for African Americans following the *Gaines* decision.

Several individuals and institutions were observing the situation at NCCU. Walter White of the NAACP assured Shepard that "under no circumstances would his Association foster and be satisfied with regional schools."[47] Al-though White argued that the NAACP was more concerned with the equal-ization of teachers' salaries at the time, he also believed that the situation in North Carolina was "unique." Though Shepard led a gallant fight, the School of Social Work never materialized at NCCU. Shepard's actions were para-mount in the overall struggle to secure advanced education in black social work. Instead, he established a Law School and School of Library Science in 1940 and 1941, respectively.[48]

Even though Jones did not play a leading role in North Carolina, his activi-ties with the NUL helped to make social work accessible to black people in the North and South. He had worked to make social work for black people a national concern in the 1910s and 1920s, and his efforts in previous decades were aided by increasing access for black men and women to the social-work profession. It may seem that Jones was not involved with the national events occurring within the profession, but other circumstances at the NUL and in his personal life claimed his immediate attention.

Jones chose not to remain in Washington during Roosevelt's second term (1936–40). As he returned to New York, the national office of the Urban League was under enormous financial stress. In addition to the overall changes in the profession, Jones lost his greatest advocate for the NUL's programs. Ruth Standish Baldwin died in 1934, leaving the major financial burden to Jones at the height of the Depression. Furthermore, the Urban League was receiving criticism from friends and foes alike by the mid-1930s. E. Franklin Frazier reported to Gunnar Myrdal that much necessary work in education was not being considered by the NUL officials: "[I]n one city where they attempted to organize a Workers' Council they invited only professional people and neglected the more intelligent and more articulate members of the working class."[49] Concern from the black working class had grown during this period.

Despite these growing tensions, Jones continued to push for an available pool of young black social workers through the NUL's fellowship training. By 1938, Charles S. Johnson of Fisk University was soliciting a list of the best candidates from the Urban League's pool of applicants. Jones stated to Johnson in June 1938 that "there were so many worthy applicants for our fellowships who could not be taken care of by us, that I had no choice but to send you their names."[50] Jones and Johnson understood that social-work credentials would be transformed in 1939, and their impatience to get the students trained is not surprising. Jones and the NUL, as well as other organizations working in the interest of African Americans, experienced a backlash from white interest groups.

Throughout the New Deal, the white South worried that continual federal activism and the emergence of a liberal coalition within the national Democratic party would undermine their way of life.[51] The historian Patricia Sullivan contends that the white South was far more concerned with the broader thrust of the New Deal than with the NAACP, fearing that the New Deal "threatened to undermine the political structure of the Solid South."[52] Such southern organizations as the Women's National Association for the Preservation of the White Race (WNAPWR) actively sought to discredit the work of the NUL. In April 1939, Mrs. J. E. Andrews of the WNAPWR wrote to another member of the organization, "We are not unfriendly to Negroes. We object to the ruin of our white children and students by them."[53] The group's motto was "The Teaching of God's Word to the Children of the Nation—the Word of God—Allegiance to the National Constitution."[54] This organization felt it had a duty to ward off what it perceived as destruction: "[W]e are organized for *PRESERVATION*—not even *ADVANCEMENT,* as the Negroes are," Andrews stated, adding, "[I]t is not we but Negroes who are seeking to deny that right [full citizenship] to others."[55] This group questioned every organization that ever came to the aid of African Americans. Andrews further claimed that continued assistance to African Americans and not whites would eventually wipe out the white race. The usual generous financial contributors of the NUL were brought into question, creating further tension within the NUL and other such groups. This was not the least of Jones's concerns.

His relationship with T. Arnold Hill had grown distant during his tenure with the New Deal. Much of the stress between Jones and Hill centered on Hill's radical and confrontational approach to the work of the NUL. The Urban League's largely liberal and white Executive Board members had grown increasingly dissatisfied with Hill's public persona in Jones's absence.[56] Guichard Parris and Lester Brooks claim that during Hill's tenure as executive secretary, "the entire tenor of the NUL had changed."[57] Hill had sought to align the league with the more vocal concerns of the labor movement in the 1930s. According to Parris and Brooks, Hill struggled with the question of whether the Urban League was to become "more radical or more conservative."[58] This is one reason why Jones was unable to participate in the many other changes occurring within the social-work profession in the late 1930s. The financial situation of the NUL had worsened, and therefore Jones focused most of his time on the New York headquarters and operational needs. Hill had attempted to push the NUL into a much more proactive role in society. Upon Jones's return in 1937, most of his attention was consumed by the immediate events within the NUL. By 1938, Jones "slammed on the brakes and the NUL reverted to a more sedate approach to black problems in the nation."[59] There were other matters of even greater concern in Jones's personal life.

Perhaps the most pressing matter for Jones was his declining health. In January 1939, he was stricken with tuberculosis. Jones took several months to recuperate.[60] During his illness, Jesse O. Thomas, the southern field director of the NUL, became acting director.[61] Thomas was cautious not to make many hasty decisions during Jones's absence, considering the climate created by Hill during Jones's stint in Washington, D.C.[62]

Jones was advised by his physician to convalesce in a more suitable climate than New York City. He was forced to choose between his career and his health. Before Jones made this important decision, an even greater decision had to be made in conjunction with the Executive Board of the NUL.

In January 1940, T. Arnold Hill hand-delivered his resignation from the NUL to Jones at his home in Flushing. Hill's decision caused much concern among his friends and colleagues around the country. Many believed that the Executive Board had treated him unfairly. Moreover, some of Hill's allies felt that Jones had not supported him and that the issue should have been taken up further with the Executive Board. Many of Jones's supporters disagreed. In the end, Hill's decision to quit the NUL after twenty-five years of service was official.[63]

Jones was faced with his own departure from the NUL, along with the major concern as to who would become the new executive secretary. Parris and Brooks question whether there was "room at the top for anyone but Jones . . . [and] if so, whom?"[64] Hill was gone, and he was not to be retrieved. Jones's diplomatic decision proved typical of his style and character. He selected Lester B. Granger, Hill's understudy and the former head of the Workers' Bureau, to be the assistant executive secretary through industrial relations. This reassured those who still wished for Hill's type of "spark and drive."[65]

Granger grew up in a black middle-class family in Newport News, Virginia. His parents were professionals—his mother a teacher and his father a doctor. Granger graduated from Dartmouth College in 1918 with a B.A. in economics and later studied at the New York School for Social Work.[66] He took over as executive secretary of the NUL on October 1, 1940, at a time of major concern for the organization.[67] It appeared to be a "seemingly hopeless situation" that Granger would set out to control during his two decades at the helm of the NUL.[68]

Before Jones departed from public work, the Swedish social economist Gunnar Myrdal interviewed him. Myrdal was commissioned by the Carnegie Corporation to study the race problem in America, and he thought it necessary to interview as many prominent Americans as possible. In 1940 he interviewed Jones about his life and his work with the NUL. The finished product, An American Dilemma, is considered a classic.[69]

Although he was a leading social-work economist, Jones's retirement from the national office of the Urban League occurred at a time of unsettling national and international events. . As he settled into his newly designed position of general secretary of the NUL by 1941, the nation was focused on A. Philip Randolph's March on Washington and World War II.

Randolph's persistent efforts on behalf of black workers consumed black America's attention.[70] Randolph's public profile grew substantially following his major victory with the establishment of the Brotherhood of Sleeping Car Porters Union in 1925.[71] Randolph particularly focused on the wartime industries and the lack of employment opportunities for African Americans, especially given that they all received government support and contracts.

In September 1940, Randolph began making plans for his March on Washington, which was to take place on July 1, 1941. Randolph, his supporters, and many in the black community convinced President Roosevelt that their intentions were serious enough that he issued Executive Order 8802, declaring, "[T]here shall be no discrimination in the employment of workers in defense industries or government because of race, creed, color, or national origin." This order led to the establishment of the Committee on Fair Employment Practices. Though this executive order only addressed federal jobs and facilities under federal jurisdiction, it set a major precedent.[72] This was one of the first victories on the road to the modern civil-rights movement. These national events occurred as Jones was handing over the leadership of the NUL to Granger in 1940. As the United States was on the brink of entering World War II, many more issues were mounting in black America. From the 1930s through the 1940s, the nation witnessed vast changes in the status of the African American social, political, and economic situation. This is the decade that many historians have termed the "the path to equality." From the Scottsboro Boys in Alabama to the breaking of baseball's color barrier by Jackie Robinson, the decade witnessed numerous changes that transformed the social, political, and economic landscape of the United States.[73]

Tuscon, Arizona, became Jones's winter residence for most of the remainder of his life.[74] Due to his failing health, he could no longer keep up with the work required to operate the NUL on a daily basis. After Granger was named executive secretary, Jones was granted the title of general secretary, a position he served for the next ten years. From 1940 to 1950, he continued to advise the Urban League on most of its activities. While he spent the winter months in Arizona, he remained in touch with practically every aspect of the NUL's business.

Jones took up residence at 516 North Granada Street in Tucson and soon engaged himself with the local activities of Arizona's Urban Leagues. By September 1944, he had arranged for the establishment of an Urban League branch in Phoenix.[75] In this way, he managed to stay involved with the national office. In 1945, the NUL prepared to observe its thirty-fifth anniversary. Jones wrote to Charles S. Johnson that the fall issue of *Opportunity* would be a special edition devoted to discussions "of the objectives and activities of the League with special emphasis on what the League has accomplished in the field of race relations and improved opportunities for Negroes."[76] Jones arranged the format of the special edition and sought Johnson's input: "We shall have six editorials of approximately four hundred words each, from such persons, we hope, as Anson Phelps Stokes, Hollingsworth Wood, and Mrs. Eleanor Roosevelt. We are particularly anxious that you and Elmer Carter, the only two editors *Opportunity* has had, write short editorials as features."[77] Johnson responded eagerly.

Jones was invited to lecture at a meeting of the Tucson Council of Social Agencies at the local YWCA on April 2, 1947. The *Arizona Daily Star* quoted him as saying that "the American Negro passes his life in an atmosphere of uncertainty."[78] Jones forwarded a copy of the newspaper clipping to his longtime friend Guichard Parris. By the late 1940s, Jones and Parris maintained a continual line of correspondence to inform each other of urban progress and the disadvantages of the African American population.

By the late 1940s, Jones's daily activities had decreased considerably. Despite his declining health, he accepted some speaking engagements and conference invitations. On June 14, 1948, he addressed the Interracial Forum of New York City, where he informed the audience that the aim of the NUL had been to work toward the "successful integration of the Negro in the life of the community, where no special privileges are extended nor any opportunities denied and the merit of the system is allowed to operate freely."[79]

The 1948 annual meeting of the NUL was held in Jones's boyhood home of Richmond, Virginia. Though he had left Richmond as a young man for college, it remained a place of great fondness for him.[80] J. Harvey Kerns, the chairman of the NUL Annual Conference Committee, wrote to inform Jones that Dr. J. M. Ellison, the president of Virginia Union University, was going to deliver the welcome address. He also informed Jones that he had been "selected by the Conference Committee to respond to the address of welcome," emphasizing "your many admirers in Richmond whom, I am sure, will be on hand to hear one of their sons."[81] Jones responded promptly to this request: "It is my plan and my hope that I shall be with you at the Conference in Richmond."[82] In July 1948, Ellison extended an invitation to Mr. and Mrs. Jones to "be our house guests as you attend the annual meeting of the National Urban League." Ellison further stated, "[W]e shall want to do all possible to make your stay pleasant while on the campus of Virginia Union, your Alma Mater, and of which you have been an honored and faithful trustee through the years."[83] Jones wrote back on July 12, 1948, thanking Ellison for the "considerate" invitation and to assure him that he and Mrs. Jones were "deeply appreciative."[84] The summer of 1948 was a busy time for Jones. The Citizens' Housing and Planning Council of New York sent him a copy of Robert Weaver's *The Negro Ghetto* in August, asking him to review it for its organizational newsletter.

Jones wrote a favorable review, claiming that Weaver "shows how the Negro in cities north and south has been shunted across the railroad track and into blighted and deserted areas by departing whites in quest of homes in suburbs and subdivisions."[85] He praised Weaver's book by proclaiming that "a thorough job has been done to give students and city planners complete data and logical arguments to forestall future schemes to withhold decent homes from America's minorities."[86] This signaled one of the last formal entreaties by Jones within the social-work profession.

In 1950, Eugene Kinckle Jones retired from the NUL and public work altogether. After his retirement, he could begin to reflect on what had been essential to the Urban League's survival. In May 1951, he declared that "progress taken from decade to decade had been tremendous"; "much of it, to his great satisfaction, resulted not from mass pressure or political compromise but from the pressure of logic, understanding, good will, and common sense."[87] At the time of Jones's retirement, he was viewed as "one of the nation's elder statesmen in better race relations."[88]

Jones died in the early morning hours of January 11, 1954, as the result of a brain aneurysm at the age of sixty-eight. He had been comatose for two weeks before passing away at his home in Flushing, New York.[89] The nation mourned the passing of this American statesman.

Conclusion

Eugene Kinckle Jones was born in racially polarized Richmond into a comfortable middle-class black family. Both of his college-educated parents were noted residents of the city. Jones grew to maturity during a period in American history in which the federal government no longer had an expressed interest in securing full citizenship rights for its black citizens. Further, the white South successfully denounced and denied Fourteenth and Fifteenth Amendment rights to blacks.

While growing up, Jones witnessed African American men and women struggling to hold on to the gains of Reconstruction. The black middle class in the late nineteenth century also assigned a peculiar level of responsibility to Jones and his peers, the Talenth Tenth. It was this understanding that Jones and his peers took on as their life missions, regardless of their chosen careers. This is the history I have sought to detail by piecing together Eugene Kinckle Jones's life work.

Jones and his peers belonged to the group of African Americans whose contributions, had it not been for their race, would have been properly acknowledged long before now. Jones has been omitted from social-work history largely because of the racial climate in which he worked. I concur with much of the recent scholarship that concludes that Jane Addams and others have occupied the single place at the top for far too long. The historian Earl E. Thorpe declared in 1984 that the Progressive Era in "black America produced its own very important Muckrakers and Progressive Movement." He further pointed out that "nationally, the best-known leaders were such persons as W. E. B. DuBois, Carter G. Woodson, George Edmund Haynes,

James Weldon Johnson, Ida Wells Barnett, Mary Church Terrell, and Eugene Kinckle Jones."[1]

The individual histories of such persons as Jones will challenge our traditional notions of social reform early in the twentieth century. A broader definition of social reform is necessary to understand the accomplishments of Addams and her African American peers. The accomplishments of African American social reformers often did not mirror those of their white counterparts due to the racial stratification of American society. This history of Jones and the rise of professional black social workers attempts to establish this broader definition of social-reform movements in the African American community.

Jones was a giant among giants within the social-reform movement. He achieved numerous distinctions in addition to the executive directorship of the NUL. He was a founding member of the nation's first black fraternity at Cornell University in 1906, and he established fellowship programs at the NUL at a time when social work for black people had not been seriously considered. He took the philosophy of the Alpha Phi Alpha fraternity into the National Urban League. Having established the first two chapters of Alpha Phi Alpha beyond Cornell, he implanted this idea of local branches with the NUL in the 1920s. Jones worked continuously during his early tenure with the NUL to establish as many local branches as possible. In 1915, he and a group of black social reformers founded the Social Work Club to address the concerns of black social work and workers. The organization was short-lived, but by 1921 black social workers were actively involved with the American Association of Social Workers. In 1925, the National Conference of Social Work elected Jones as the first African American to its Executive Board as treasurer. He went on to serve the organization for the next six years. By 1933, he had risen to the prominent position of vice president of the NCSW. During his tenure as an executive officer, he worked along with other black social workers to make known their concerns and those of urban black people in general.

Jones became one the most important advocates for jobs for African Americans during the Great Depression. He worked directly with the Department of Commerce as the Advisor on Negro Affairs. No one worked harder than Jones to publicize within the African American community the available opportunities through newly initiated federal relief programs. He also served as the black community's voice through the NUL's local branches. He continued to personify the NUL while he served in Washington from 1933 to 1936.

This study makes clear that Jones was the nationally visible representative of the NUL who laid the foundation for future executive secretaries. During his tenure, the NUL became an American institution. George Edmund Haynes was the first executive secretary of the Urban League, but his stint with the organization was too brief to accomplish the lasting impact that Jones did. At the time of Jones's death in 1954, the NUL was intricately woven into the fabric of American culture and society. Though it would be another decade or two before the Urban League began to engage in direct confrontations of the civil-rights movement, through Jones's efforts it was firmly established as a useful organization.

Notes

Introduction

1. Parris and Brooks, *Blacks in the City,* ix.

2. Thorpe, *Concise History of North Carolina Central University,* 73.

Chapter 1. From Richmond to Ithaca

1. *Abridged Autobiography of Eugene Kinckle Jones,* dictated to Gunnar Myrdal, 1940, p. 1, NUL Papers, Collections of the Manuscript Division, Library of Congress, Washington, D.C. See also Simmons, *Men of Mark,* 234–39.

2. Dabney, *Richmond,* 262–64. The lineage of Sicily Jones was confirmed in my interview with Betty Jones Dowling, Jones's granddaughter, in June 1995, Washington, D.C. The family has photographs of the gravesite of Sicily Jones.

3. Litwack, *Been in the Storm So Long,* 167–68. See also Harding, *There Is a River,* 275.

4. Harding, *There Is a River,* 274.

5. See Simmons, *Men of Mark,* 234–39; and Corey, *History of the Richmond Theological Seminary,* 173–78.

6. See Corey, *History of Richmond Theological Seminary*; Rabinowitz, *Race Relations in the Urban South,* 163; Anderson, *Education of Blacks in the South*; and Rachleff, *Black Labor in Richmond.*

7. *Abridged Autobiography of Eugene Kinckle Jones,* 10. My account of Jones's early life has been pieced together through this document in conjunction with Scruggs, *Women of Distinction.* Scruggs provides a biographical sketch of Rosa Kinckle Jones, describing her as "one of [Richmond's] most prominent, if not the most prominent and successful teacher of music, having taught some who are now successful teachers themselves." E. K. Jones's granddaughter, Betty Jones Dowling, confirmed much of this information during our June 1995 interview. An "express business" is the system for the prompt and safe

transportation of parcels, money, or goods at rates higher than standard freight charges or a company operating such a merchandise-freight service

8. *City Directory of Lynchburg, Virginia*, 1879–80, p. 119; 1881–82, p. 103; 1887–88, p. 131, Virginia State Library and Archives, Richmond.

9. For a discussion of black life in Richmond and Norfolk, see Lewis, Earl, *In Their Own Interests*; and Brown, "Uncle Ned's Children."

10. Litwack, *Been in the Storm So Long*, 313; Rabinowitz, *Race Relations in the Urban South*, 12–13.

11. Rachleff, *Black Labor in Richmond*, 14–15.

12. Engs, *Freedom's First Generation*, xx.

13. Harding, *There Is a River*, 297. Harding appropriately titles this chapter, "The Challenge of the Children."

14. Dabney, *Richmond*, 198; Rabinowitz, *Race Relations in the Urban South*, 13. See also, Taylor, *Negro in the Reconstruction of Virginia*.

15. Qtd. in *Abridged Autobiography of Eugene Kinckle Jones*, 10

16. Parris and Brooks, *Blacks in the City*, 156–57.

17. Gatewood, *Aristocrats of Color*, 70. Chapter 3 includes Gatewood's detailed analysis of elite blacks in the South. Perhaps his shortcoming is that he singled out such cities as Washington, Baltimore, New Orleans, and Charleston, South Carolina, as prime examples of this group while ignoring Richmond, which clearly was at the center of similar activity in the South during this time.

18. Gaines, *Uplifting the Race*.

19. Taylor, *Negro in the Reconstruction of Virginia*, 191–92; Simmons, *Men of Mark*, 234–39.

20. Kornweibel, *No Crystal Stair*, 24–25. See also Anderson, *Education of Blacks in the South*; and Harlan, *Booker T. Washington*.

21. Logan, *Howard University*, 97–98; Simmons, *Men of Mark*, 234–39.

22. *Abridged Autobiography of Eugene Kinckle Jones*; Scruggs, *Women of Distinction*, 337–39.

23. Chesson, *Richmond after the War*, 194–95.

24. *The Messenger*, 1921, 15.

25. Ibid.

26. Ibid. Hartshorn celebrated its fortieth year of operation in 1921, when this article was published. Mrs. Rosa Jones was no longer affiliated with the school at this time, but the article indicates the type of education that Hartshorn had provided for African American girls. See also Shaw, *What a Woman Ought to Be and to Do*, 85–87; and Logan, *Howard University*, 97.

27. Logan, *Howard University*, 97.

28. *Richmond City Directory*, 1896, Virginia State Library and Archives, Richmond. By 1896 the Joneses were both listed with professional titles: Rosa as a teacher at Hartshorn Memorial College, and Joseph as a teacher at Richmond Theological Seminary. Eugene Kinckle Jones's student records for Cornell University reveal his permanent address for Richmond. Eugene Kinckle Jones Alumni Folder, Cornell University Rare and Manuscript Collections, University Library, Ithaca, N.Y.

29. Rabinowitz, *Race Relations in the Urban South*, 98.

30. Ibid., 37–38

31. Wynes, *Race Relations in Virginia,* 16. For a general discussion of how the Republican party lost its battle in the South during Reconstruction, see Moneyhon, "Failure of Southern Republicanism."

32. Painter, *Standing at Armageddon,* 1.

33. Chesson, "Richmond's Black Councilmen," 191.

34. Ibid.

35. Rabinowitz, *Race Relations in the Urban South,* 105.

36. See Logan, *Negro in American Life and Thought*; Rabinowitz, *Race Relations in the Urban South*; and Chesson, *Richmond after the War.*

37. Chesson, "Richmond's Black Councilmen," 192; Chesson, *Richmond after the War,* 195–96.

38. Rabinowitz, *Race Relations in the Urban South,* 98.

39. U. S. Bureau of the Census, *Compendium of the Eleventh Census, 1890,* vol. 1 (Washington, D.C.: Government Printing Office, 1896), 850. See also Chesson, *Richmond after the War,* 191–92; and Rabinowitz, *Race Relations in the Urban South.*

40. Rabinowitz, *Race Relations in the Urban South,* 98.

41. Dabney, *Richmond,* 241.

42. Ibid.

43. Ibid., 242. For further discussion of Mitchell and the other black city councilmen in Richmond during this era, see Chesson, "Richmond's Black Councilmen"; and Chesson, *Richmond after the War.*

44. Chesson, *Richmond after the War,* 195. See also Work Projects Administration of Virginia, *Negro in Virginia.*

45. Ibid., 242

46. Ovington, *Portraits in Color,* 146.

47. Moss, *American Negro Academy,* 27, 29, 36, and introduction. For more detailed discussion of Joseph Jones's life and career, see Simmons, *Men of Mark,* 234–39; and Gavins, *Perils and Prospects of Southern Black Leadership,* 24–25.

48. Moss, *American Negro Academy,* 27.

49. *Abridged Autobiography of Eugene Kinckle Jones,* 2.

50. See Brown, "Womanish Consciousness"; Chesson, *Richmond after the War,* 194; and Hammond, *In the Vanguard of a Race,* 108–18.

51. Meier, *Negro Thought in America,* 15.

52. Brown, "Uncle Ned's Children," 2.

53. Rachleff, *Black Labor in Richmond,* 158.

54. *Abridged Autobiography of Eugene Kinckle Jones,* 2–3.

55. Ibid.

56. Ibid.

57. Ibid., 3.

58. Gavins, *Perils and Prospects of Southern Black Leadership,* 23.

59. Rachleff, *Black Labor in Richmond,* 23–24. For a discussion of Booker T. Washington and the Industrial Educational Model, see Harlan, *Booker T. Washington: The Wizard of Tuskegee*; Meier, *Negro Thought in America,* 207–47. See also Anderson, *Education of Blacks in the South*; and Anderson, "Hampton Model of Normal School Industrial Education."

60. Meier, *Negro Thought in America,* 175–78.

61. Ibid.

62. Ibid., 5. For further discussion of the southern black aristocrats, see Gatewood, *Aristocrats of Color,* chap. 3.

63. See Wesley, "Graduate Education for Negroes in Southern Universities," 82–83; and Anderson, *Education of Blacks in the South.*

64. Bishop, *History of Cornell,* 274–76.

65. Ovington, *Portraits in Color,* 136–85.

66. Eugene Kinckle Jones to Prof. W. E. B. DuBois, Atlanta University, April 24, 1907, The Papers of W. E. B. DuBois, 1877–1963, reel 2, frame 287, Microfilm, Michigan State University, East Lansing.

67. Eugene Kinckle Jones to Prof. W. E. B. DuBois, Atlanta University, ibid. See also Lewis, *W. E. B. DuBois.*

68. *Abridged Autobiography of Eugene Kinckle Jones,* 2.

69. Fireside, *Plessy v. Ferguson,* 5–6.

70. Ibid.

71. Jones's address can be found in his correspondence.

72. Wesley, *History of Alpha Phi Alpha,* 15.

73. Eugene Kinckle Jones Alumni Folder, Rare and Manuscript Collections, University Library, Cornell University, Ithaca.

74. See Ayers, *Promise of the New South.*

75. Ibid., xiii; Wesley, "Graduate Education for Negroes in Southern Universities," 82–83. Wesley does an excellent job of painting the segregated nature of life at the turn of the century for black Americans. He also singles out the fact that many black students at Cornell were from middle-class backgrounds and that their plight was characterized by Jim Crow proscriptions. Even higher-class status did not make them immune to racial segregation and discrimination.

76. Wesley, *Henry Arthur Callis,* 276. Callis was a founding member, with Jones, of the fraternity. After completing his work at Cornell, Callis enrolled in Howard University's School of Medicine, eventually fulfilling his lifelong dream to become a doctor and address the concerns of black health care. Wesley's book compiles all of his medical writings.

77. Ibid., 277.

78. Wesley, *History of Alpha Phi Alpha,* xiii.

79. *Abridged Autobiography of Eugene Kinckle Jones,* 6–7.

80. Wesley, *Henry Arthur Callis,* 281. For a detailed discussion of Mary Church Terrell, see Harley, "Mary Church Terrell"; Terrell, *Colored Woman in a White World;* and Jones, *Quest for Equality.*

81. Wesley, *Henry Arthur Callis,* xvii. See also Lewis, *W. E. B. DuBois,* 350–54; and Rudwick, "W. E. B. DuBois as Sociologist."

82. *Abridged Autobiography of Eugene Kinckle Jones,* 7.

83. Ibid., xvi.

84. Gatewood, *Black Americans and the White Man's Burden,* 2–3.

85. Jones, Butler, "Tradition of Sociology Teaching in Black Colleges."

86. E. E. Pratt to A. Clayton Powell Sr., April 12, 1911, George E. Haynes Papers, box 2, folder 7, Fisk Univesity Archives, Nashville.

Chapter 2. Building Alliances

1. Ehrenreich, *Altruistic Imagination*, 57–58.

2. Jones, Eugene Kinkle, "Social Work among Negroes," *The Messenger*, 27. *The Messenger*, produced by Chandler Owens and A. Philip Randolph, was the most radical black journal of the early twentieth century. See Kornweibel, *No Crystal Stair*; and Pfeffer, *A. Philip Randolph*.

3. For a discussion of how social work was used to exercise some sense of social order, see Crocker, *Social Work and Social Order*. See also Lasch-Quinn, *Black Neighbors*.

4. Ehrenreich, *Altruistic Imagination*, 57–58.

5. For a look at early social-work activities, see Devine, *When Social Work Was Young*, esp. chap. 3; and Ferguson. *Social Work*. For a more in-depth understanding of social work and other professions in the early twentieth century, see Larson, *Rise of Professionalism*.

6. Fisher, *Response of Social Work to the Depression*.

7. Lasch-Quinn, *Black Neighbors*. Lasch-Quinn argues that white settlement-house workers were not willing to open their settlements to southern migrant blacks, and when they did, it was only on a limited basis. Even such noted reformers as Edith Abbott, Jane Addams, and Sophonisba Breckinridge subscribed to the laws of Jim Crow. See Trolander, *Professionalism and Social Change*, 93–95.

8. *Historical Statistics of the United States*, 105. See also Henri, *Black Migration*, 49–53.

9. Lash-Quinn, *Black Neighbors*; Crocker, *Social Work and Social Order*; Trolander, *Settlement Houses and the Great Depression*.

10. Katz, *In the Shadow of the Poorhouse*, 177.

11. Ibid.

12. Henri, *Black Migration*, 53.

13. See Trotter, *Great Migration in Historical Perspective*. Two of the more prominent regional works on black migration are Gottlieb, *Making Their Own Way*; and Grossman, *Land of Hope*. See also Sherman, *Negro and the City*; and Johnson, *Black Manhattan*.

14. See Painter, *Exodusters*.

15. Sherman, *Negro and the City*, 6–13; Marks, *Farewell—We're Good and Gone*.

16. Marks, "Social and Economic Life of Southern Blacks during the Migration," 40–41.

17. Ibid., 41–42.

18. Sherman, *Negro and the City*, 6–13. For a discussion of the *Chicago Defender*, see Grossman, *Land of Hope*. See also Hine, "Black Migration to the Urban Midwest."

19. Sherman, *Negro and the City*, 6–14.

20. Handlin, *Newcomers*. On restrictive covenants, see Lynch, *Black Urban Condition*; Taeuber and Taeuber, *Negroes in Cities*; and Vose, *Caucasians Only*.

21. "Race Segregation Is in Violation of Federal Constitution, U. S. Supreme Court Holds," *New York Times*, November 6, 1917, 18.

22. Biskupic and Witt, *Congressional Quarterly's Guide to the U. S. Supreme Court*, 898. See also Vose, *Caucasians Only*.

23. See Rudwick, *Race Riot at East St. Louis*; Tuttle, *Race Riot*; Ellsworth, *Death in the Promised Land*; Senechal, *Sociogenesis of a Race Riot*; and Hendricks, "Politics of Race," 190–224.

24. Jones, Eugene Kinkle, "Social Work among Negroes," *The Messenger*, 287.

25. Fogel, "Social Work and Negroes," *The Messenger*, 281.

26. For a complete study of the founding the NUL, see Weiss, *National Urban League*.

27. Ibid., chaps. 2 and 3.

28. Carlton-LaNey, "Training African-American Social Workers through the NUL Fellowship Program," 43.

29. Ibid., 44–45.

30. Chambers, *Seedtime of Reform*. Chambers is the senior social-work historian in the United States. He laid the groundwork on the history of social work with major works such as *The New Deal at Home and Abroad* and *Paul U. Kellogg and the* Survey. (These will be discussed in detail in chapter 3.) Chambers falls short of including the role of black people in this history.

31. Trolander, *Settlement Houses and the Great Depression*, 15.

32. W. E. B. DuBois to Eugene Kinckle Jones, April 10, 1918, NUL Papers, Miscellaneous Items, Library of Congress, Washington, D.C.

33. Eugene Kinckle Jones to Dr. W. E. B. DuBois, April 5, 1918, NUL Papers, Miscellaneous Items, Library of Congress, Washington, D.C. For a further study of Adah B. Thoms, a founding member of the National Association of Colored Graduate Nurses, see Thoms, *Pathfinders*; and Hine, *Black Women in White*.

34. Gary and Gary, "History of Social Work Education for Black People," 67–70.

35. Ibid., 74.

36. Richardson, *History of Fisk University*, 1–12. See also Welch, "The Background and Development of the American Missionary Association's Decision to Educate Freedmen in the South," 93–146; and Smith, "Sociological Research and Fisk University."

37. Weiss, *National Urban League*, 33–34.

38. *Opportunity* (May 1923): 4.

39. Meier, Elizabeth, *History of the New York School of Social Work*, 3–9. While Meier's work is considered a comprehensive history of the New York School of Social Work, it does not offer anything about the training of black social workers. For an understanding of New York School of Social Work and its disposition, a study of *Opportunity* and its annual reports, which were done by Jones, proves to be revealing.

40. Richardson, *History of Fisk University*, 64, 75; and author's interview with Francis Kornegay, 1994, Detroit. Dr. Kornegay provided recollections of Eugene Kinckle Jones, who was still alive when he first joined the Detroit branch of the Urban League and was a friend of Kornegay. Weiss, *National Urban League*. For an in-depth study of George Edmund Haynes's role in the professionalization of black social workers, see Perlman, "Stirring the White Conscience," chap. 4. See also Jones, Butler, "Tradition of Sociology Teaching in Black Colleges."

41. Eugene Kinckle Jones to Prof. W. E. B. DuBois, Atlanta University, February 5, 1908, Papers of W. E. B. DuBois, 1877–1963, Reel 2, Frame 287, Microfilm, Michigan State University, East Lansing. In this letter, Jones inquires about some statistical information on the health of the American Negro.

42. *Opportunity* (May 1923): 31. Jones, Eugene Kinckle, "Negro's Struggle for Health."

43. *Opportunity* (July 1926): 230.

44. Sitkoff, *New Deal for Blacks*, 24.

45. Jones, Eugene Kinckle, "Some Fundamental Factors in Regard to the Health of the Negro," 176–78.

46. Jones, Eugene Kinckle, "The Negro in Community Life," 388.

47. "Social Service Progress in 1926," p. 1, NUL Papers, Collections of the Manuscript Division, Library of Congress, Washington, D.C. .

48. Ibid.

49. Ibid.

50. *Abridged Autobiography of Eugene Kinckle Jones.*

51. Ibid.

52. Lasch-Quinn, *Black Neighbors.*

53. Katz, *In the Shadow of the Poorhouse,* 177.

Chapter 3. An Era of National Conflict and Cooperation

1. *Abridged Autobiography of Eugene Kinckle Jones,* dictated to Gunnar Myrdal, 1940, pp. 3–4, NUL Papers, Collections of the Manuscript Division, Library of Congress, Washington, D.C.

2. "Kinckle Jones Report," editorial, *New York Times,* April 27, 1932.

3. Weiss, *National Urban League,* 83–92

4. Goggin, *Carter G. Woodson,* 56. Eugene Kinckle Jones to Alfred Stern, Director of the Julius Rosenwald Fund, April 16, 1928, Julius Rosenwald Fund Archives, box 306, folder 9, Amistad Research Center, Tulane University, New Orleans. See also, Hine, "Carter G. Woodson"; and McMurry, *Recorder of the Black Experience.*

5. Goggin, *Carter G. Woodson,* 58.

6. Alfred Stern to Eugene Kinckle Jones, January 10, 1928, and reply, April 16, 1928, Julius Rosenwald Fund Archives, box 306, folder 9, Amistad Research Center, Tulane University, New Orleans. Though the letters are dated 1928—after the five-and-a-half-year period was up—it is clear that this was the reason Jones began to solicit the Rosenwald Fund to continue to finance the NUL. See Weiss, *National Urban League.*

7. For an in-depth study of *Opportunity* and its role in the Harlem Renaissance, see Lewis, *When Harlem Was in Vogue,* chap. 7. See also Wintz, *Black Culture and the Harlem Renaissance*; and Robbins, "Charles S. Johnson."

8. Lewis, *W. E. B. DuBois.* See also Weiss, *National Urban League,* chap. 4.

9. Jones, Butler, "Tradition of Sociology Teaching in Black Colleges"; Ross, *Black Heritage in Social Welfare.*

10. Ross, *Black Heritage in Social Welfare,* 423–25; Blackwell and Janowitz, *Black Sociologists.* For a complete study of E. Franklin Frazier, see Platt, *E. Franklin Frazier Reconsidered.* For a listing of some of the works compiled by Frazier, see *Negro Family in the United States*; *Black Bourgeoisie*; and *Negro Race in Chicago.* The most provocative work done by Charles S. Johnson is *Negro in Chicago.*

11. Crocker, *Social Work and Social Order,* 6. See also Knight, "Jane Addams and the Settlement House Movement."

12. Williams, "Social Bonds in the 'Black Belt' of Chicago." See also, Knupfer, *Toward a Tenderer Humanity and a Nobler Womanhood.*

13. Carlton-LaNey, "Elizabeth Ross Haynes," 1.

14. Giddings, *When and Where I Enter,* 142–47.

15. See Jones, Adrienne, *Jane Edna Hunter.* For a discussion of W. Gertrude Brown, see

Trolander, *Settlement Houses and the Great Depression,* chap. 9. For a detailed study of Haynes's life and career, see Carlton-LaNey, "Career of Birdye Henrietta Haynes"; Shaw, *What a Woman Ought to Be and to Do*; and Cromwell, "Black Women as Pioneers in Social Welfare," 7–12.

16. Neverdon-Morton, *Afro-American Women of the South and the Advancement of the Race,* 8.

17. Walkowitz, "Making of a Feminine Professional Identity," 1051–53. See also Chambers, "Women in the Creation of the Profession of Social Work"; and Popple, "Social Work Profession."

18. Walkowitz, "Making of a Feminine Professional Identity," 1053.

19. Carlton-LaNey, "Career of Birdye Henrietta Haynes," 254.

20. Chambers, "Women in the Creation of the Profession of Social Work." Chambers lists such noted white social workers as Edward Devine, Homer Folks, Paul U. Kellogg, Graham Taylor, Jane Addams, Mary Richmond, Lillian Wald, Edith Abbott, Sophonisba Breckinridge, and Mary Van Kleeck.

21. Cromwell, "Black Women as Pioneers in Social Welfare," 11.

22. Johnson, "The Sin of Omission: African-American Women in Social Work."

23. Gamble, *Making a Place for Ourselves,* xvii.

24. Chafe, "Women's History and Political History," 106.

25. Carlton-LaNey, "Career of Birdye Henrietta Haynes," 269.

26. Kogut. "Negro and the Charity Organization Society in the Progressive Era." Fannie Barrier Williams had carried out the duties of social work in Chicago as early as 1904 when she served as the director of the Frederick Douglass Center and the Trinity Mission Settlement, which served the black population. Williams also published a provocative essay, "Social Bonds in the 'Black Belt' of Chicago." Jones's commitment to young social workers, male and female, is evident through an examination of the NUL papers at the Library of Congress. The original applications of interested individuals were all submitted with photographs.

27. Chafe, "Women's History and Political History," 114.

28. Greene. *Selling Black History for Carter G. Woodson,* 4.

29. Jones, Eugene Kinckle, review of *The Negro in Our History,* 722; Sinnette, *Arthur Alfonso Schomburg,* 126–27. See also Woodson, *Negro in Our History.* Charles H. Wesley later revised and enlarged editions of Woodson's book.

30. Jones, Eugene Kinckle, review of *The Negro in Our History,* 722.

31. Sinnette, *Arthur Alfonso Schomburg,* 127.

32. Ibid., 136–37.

33. Ibid., 171.

34. Eugene Kinckle Jones to Alfred Stern, April 16, 1928, Juilius Rosenwald Fund Archives, box 306, folder 9, Amistad Research Center, Tulane University, New Orleans. In this letter, Jones maps out to Stern the financial status of the Urban League and lists the contributing organizations and institutions. The Carnegie monies had run out, and Jones needed financial support for the Department of Research and Investigation. He had hoped to convince Stern that the NUL was worthy of the Rosenwald Fund's support now that Carnegie had declined to renew its allocations. See also Lewis, *When Harlem Was in Vogue,* 198–99; and Weiss, *National Urban League.*

35. Jones, Eugene Kinckle, "Go to High School, Go to College." See also Wesley, *History of Alpha Phi Alpha*, 103–264.

36. Eugene Kinckle Jones Alumni Folder, Cornell University Library, Rare and Manuscript Collections, Ithaca, N.Y. My interview with Jones's granddaughter, Betty Jones Dowling, confirms much of this information. She told of how the family did not break its ties to Richmond until after her grandfather's death. The family made frequent trips to Richmond, including an annual ritual of attending Virginia Union University's homecoming festivities. Eugene Kinckle Jones would typically address an audience on Founder's Day, which occurred during homecoming.

37. Jones, Eugene Kinckle, "Negro's Opportunity Today."

38. Ibid.

39. Chambers, *Paul U. Kellogg and the* Survey, 9–10.

40. Ibid., 93.

41. *Abridged Autobiography of Eugene Kinckle Jones,* 10.

42. Jones, Eugene Kinckle, "Social Work among Negroes," 287–93.

43. Ibid. See also McNeil, *Groundwork*; Thoms, *Pathfinders*; Hine, *Black Women in White*; McMurry, *George Washington Carver*; Manning, *Black Apollo of Science*; and Meier and Rudwick, *Black History and the Historical Profession.*

44. See McNeil, *Groundwork,* 6.

45. Hine, *Black Women in White,* 94. See also Hine, "'They Shall Mount Up with Wings as Eagles.'"

46. Lasch-Quinn, *Black Neighbors*; Carlton-LaNey, "Career of Birdye Henrietta Haynes."

47. Eugene K. Jones to S. A. Allen, Boston, July 28, 1926, "Race Relations," NUL Papers, series IV, box 3, Collections of the Manuscript Division, Library of Congress, Washington, D.C.

48. Ibid.

49. Ibid. See also Gary and Gary, "History of Social Work Education for Black People."

50. *Abridged Autobiography of Eugene Kinckle Jones,* 4.

51. Ibid. For a further study of how the Chicago Urban League functioned, see Grossman, *Land of Hope,* chap. 7. Grossman details the unfulfilled promises of the Urban League and the often misguided hopes for employment on the part of African Americans.

52. Gottlieb, "Rethinking the Great Migration," 74.

53. Grossman, *Land of Hope,* 145. See also Gottlieb, "White Man's Union."

54. Kusmer, *Ghetto Takes Shape,* 256.

55. Neverdon-Morton, *Afro-American Women of the South and the Advancement of the Race,* 162–63.

56. Rouse, *Lugenia Burns Hope,* 118.

57. Katzman, *Before the Ghetto.*

58. Thomas, *Life for Us Is What We Make It,* 53.

59. Ibid., 62–69. See also Dancy, *Sand against the Wind.*

60. Meier and Rudwick, *Black Detroit and the Rise of the UAW,* 18.

61. Thomas, *Life for Us Is What We Make It,* 277.

62. See Katzman, *Before the Ghetto.*

63. Meier and Rudwick, *Black Detroit and the Rise of the UAW,* 4. See also Thomas, *Life for Us Is What We Make It,* 277–312.

64. Foner, Phillip, *Organized Labor and the Black Worker*, 47. See also Weaver, *Negro Labor*; and Harris, *Harder We Run*.

65. Ibid., 174.

66. Karl R. Phillips, Commissioner of Conciliation, Correspondence, December 1924–March 1926, RG-183, No. 1400, National Archives, Washington, D.C.

Chapter 4. Between New York and Washington

1. Blum, *Progressive Presidents*.

2. Cohen, "Great Migration as a Lever for Social Change"; Parris and Brooks, *Blacks in the City*, 100–108. See also Perlman, "Stirring the White Conscience."

3. Ives, "Giles Beecher Jackson," 480. Ives is the great-granddaughter of Giles B. Jackson. See also Jackson and Davis, *Industrial History of the Negro Race of the United States*.

4. W. E. B. DuBois to Eugene Kinckle Jones, April 19, 1918, The Papers of W. E. B. DuBois, 1877–1963, reel 2, frame 287, Microfilm, Michigan State University, East Lansing.

5. Eugene Kinckle Jones to Dr. W. E. B. DuBois, April 20, 1918, The Papers of W. E. B. DuBois, 1877–1963, reel 2, frame 287, Microfilm, Michigan State University, East Lansing.

6. Julius Rosenwald (signed E. C. Scott) to Eugene Kinckle Jones, March 29, 1929, Rosenwald Fund Archives, box 306, folder 9, Amistad Research Center, Tulane University, New Orleans.

7. Edwin R. Embree, president of Julius Rosenwald Fund, to Eugene Kinckle Jones, April 4, 1929, Rosenwald Fund Archives, box 306, folder 9, Amistad Research Center, Tulane University, New Orleans.

8. Eugene Kinckle Jones to Mr. Edwin Embree, April 6, 1929, Rosenwald Fund Archives, box 306, folder 9, Amistad Research Center, Tulane University, New Orleans.

9. Ibid.

10. Eugene Kinckle Jones to Mr. Edwin R. Embree, April 27, 1929, Rosenwald Fund Archives, box 306, folder 9, Amistad Research Center, Tulane University, New Orleans.

11. Ibid.

12. Ibid.

13. Ibid.

14. Hine, "The Housewives' League of Detroit," 129.

15. President Hoover to Mr. Eugene Kinckle Jones, April 1, 1929, Rosenwald Fund Archives, box 306, folder 9, Amistad Research Center, Tulane University, New Orleans.

16. See Lasch-Quinn, *Black Neighbors*.

17. Wesley, *Negro Labor in the United States*; Jacobson, *Negro and the American Labor Movement*; Weaver, *Negro Labor*; Harris, *Harder We Run*; Spero and Harris, *Black Worker*.

18. Parris and Brooks, *Blacks in the City*, 156.

19. Hamilton, "National Urban League during the Depression," 62–63; Harris, *Keeping the Faith*, 21–25. See also Weiss, *National Urban League*; and Parris and Brooks, *Blacks in the City*, 185.

20. Strickland, *History of the Chicago Urban League*, 26–28. See also Weiss, *National Urban League*, 176–201; and Moore, *Search for Equality*, 66–67.

21. Tuttle, *Race Riot*, 61; Johnson, *Negro in Chicago*. See also Strickland, *History of the Chicago Urban League*.

22. Tuttle, *Race Riot,* 23.

23. "The Octopus and Its Tentacles," NUL Papers, series IV, box Miscellaneous, Collections of the Manuscript Division, Library of Congress, Washington, D.C.

24. Ibid.

25. Eugene Kinckle Jones to Julius Rosenwald Fund, January 2, 1930, Rosenwald Fund Archives, box 306, folder 9, Amistad Research Center, Tulane University, New Orleans.

26. Sitkoff, *New Deal for Blacks,* 24.

27. Ibid. See also Hill, Arnold, "Labor."

28. Sitkoff, *New Deal for Blacks,* 24.

29. Eugene Kinckle Jones to the Julius Rosenwald Fund, January 22, 1930, Rosenwald Fund Archives, box 306, folder 9, Amistad Research Center, Tulane University, New Orleans.

30. Eugene Kinckle Jones to Mr. George R. Arthur, the Julius Rosenwald Fund, July 2, 1931, Rosenwald Fund Archives, box 306, folder 9, Amistad Research Center, Tulane University, New Orleans.

31. George R. Arthur to Eugene Kinckle Jones, July 7, 1931, Rosenwald Fund Archives, box 306, folder 9, Amistad Research Center, Tulane University, New Orleans.

32. Eugene Kinckle Jones to Mr. Edwin R. Embree, Julius Rosenwald Fund, October 17, 1931, Rosenwald Fund Archives, box 306, folder 9, Amistad Research Center, Tulane University, New Orleans.

33. *New York Times,* editorial, February 11, 1932.

34. Eugene Kinckle Jones to the Hon. Franklin D. Roosevelt, April 15, 1935, RG 48, box 506, Department of the Interior, Office of the Secretary, National Archives, Washington, D.C.

35. Ibid.

36. Eugene Kinckle Jones to Mr. Edwin R. Embree, President of the Julius Rosenwald Fund, July 28, 1933, Rosenwald Fund Archives, box 306, folder 10, Amistad Research Center, Tulane University, New Orleans.

37. Edwin R. Embree to Eugene Kinckle Jones, August 1, 1933, Rosenwald Fund Archives, box 306, folder 10, Amistad Research Center, Tulane University, New Orleans.

38. Ibid.

39. Ibid.

40. Eugene Kinckle Jones to Edwin R. Embree, August 4, 1933, Rosenwald Fund Archives, box 306, folder 10, Amistad Research Center, Tulane University, New Orleans.

41. Ibid.

42. Parris and Brooks, *Blacks in the City,* 235.

43. *New York Times,* editorial, October 18, 1933.

44. Ibid.

45. Weiss, *National Urban League,* 269.

46. *New York Times,* editorial, May 6, 1936.

47. Goggin, *Carter G. Woodson,* 175.

48. Ibid., 176.

49. Ibid., 175. See also Ross, "Mary McLeod Bethune and the National Youth Administration"; Holt, *Mary McLeod Bethune.*

50. Jesse O. Thomas to Eugene Kinckle Jones, December 16, 1933, National Urban League, RG 48, box 83, file—Colored Work, Interracial Correspondence, CWA General

Administration/Inquiries, National Archives, Washington, D.C. See also Martin and Martin, *Social Work and the Black Experience,* 31–32.

51. Ibid.

52. Ibid.

53. Weiss, *Farewell to the Party of Lincoln,* 49–50

54. Chambers, *New Deal at Home and Abroad,* 75.

55. Ibid.

56. Ware, *Beyond Suffrage,* 12.

57. Ibid.

58. Ibid., 13. For a detailed discussion of Mary McLeod Bethune's role in the government during the New Deal, see Ross, "Mary McLeod Bethune and the National Youth Administration"; and Weiss, *Farewell to the Party of Lincoln.* For a detailed discussion of Frances Perkins, see Ware, *Beyond Suffrage;* and Ware, *Holding Their Own,* esp. chap. 4.

59. Sitkoff, *New Deal for Blacks,* 58.

60. Ibid., 59.

61. Ibid., 58.

62. Ibid., 77. See also Kirby, *Black Americans in the Roosevelt Era,* 106–7.

63. Sullivan, "Southern Reformers, the New Deal, and the Movement's Foundation," 82–83. See also Salmond, *Southern Rebel.*

64. Sitkoff, *New Deal for Blacks,* 78.

65. Harris, *Harder We Run,* 109. See also Kirby, *Black Americans in the Roosevelt Era,* esp. chap. 6.

66. Ibid.

67. Ibid., 78–79. See also Pickens, *Bursting Bonds;* Avery, *Up from Washington;* and Chambers, *Paul U. Kellogg and the Survey.*

68. Sullivan, "Southern Reformers, the New Deal, and the Movement's Foundation," 82.

69. Minutes of Inter-Departmental Group Meeting, February 7, 1934, RG 48, Central Classified File, 1907–1936, National Archives, Washington, D.C.

70. Ibid.

71. Ibid.

72. Ibid.

73. Ibid.

74. Ibid.

75. Fisher, *Response of Social Work to the Depression,* 133. For an overview of black Americans during the Depression, see Hine, *Path to Equality,* 33–47.

76. Ibid.

77. Abbott, *From Relief to Social Security,* 199 n.2. See also Lubove, *Struggle for Social Security.*

78. Abbott, *From Relief to Social Security,* 200.

79. Weiss, *National Urban League,* 275.

80. Ibid., 275.

81. Ibid, 275–76.

82. See ibid.; and Sitkoff, *New Deal for Blacks.*

83. Wye, "New Deal and the Negro Community," 621.

84. Eugene Kinckle Jones, "Summary of Work," April 1 to June 30, 1935, Department of Commerce, General Files, file 88449, box 683, National Archives, Washington, D.C.

85. Ibid.

86. Ibid.

87. "Memorandum" for Eugene Kinckle Jones, from Chester H. McCall, July 12, 1935, Department of Commerce, General File, file 88449, box 683, National Archives, Washington, D.C.

88. Secretary of Commerce Daniel C. Roper to to Mr. William W. Sanders, Executive Secretary of the National Association of Teachers, October 31, 1935, Department of Commerce, General File, file 88449, box 683, National Archives, Washington, D.C.

89. Eugene Kinckle Jones, "Summary of Work," April 1, 1936, to June 30, 1936, Department of Commerce, General File, file 88449, box 683, National Archives, Washington, D.C.

90. Ibid.

91. Ibid.

92. Sitkoff, *Struggle for Black Equality,* 10–11.

93. Ibid.

94. Eugene Kinckle Jones to Dr. W. E. B. DuBois, October 11, 1935, NUL Papers, series 5, box 8, Collections of the Manuscript Division, Library of Congress, Washington, D.C.

95. Rayford W. Logan to Eugene Kinckle Jones, November 12, 1936, NUL Papers, series 5, box 8, Collections of the Manuscript Division, Library of Congress, Washington, D.C.

96. "Memorandum" for Mr. Joseph R. Houchins, Assistant Business Specialist, Negro Affairs Division, Bureau of Foreign and Domestic Commerce, from E. W. Libbey, Chief Clerk, Department of Commerce, General Files, file 88449, box 683, National Archives, Washington, D.C.

97. Daniel C. Roper, Secretary of Commerce, to Honorable James A. Farley, chairman, Democratic National Committee, August 12, 1937, Department of Commerce, General Files, file 88449, box 683, National Archives, Washington, D.C.

98. Ibid.

99. Ibid.

Chapter 5. Changing of the Guard

1. Brown, *Public Relief.*

2. Ehrenreich, *Altruistic Imagination,* 121.

3. Ibid.

4. Trolander, *Professionalism and Social Change,* 25. See also Addams, *Twenty Years at Hull-House.*

5. Lasch-Quinn, *Black Neighbors,* 8.

6. Fisher, *Response of Social Work to the Depression,* 102. See also Spano, *Rank and File Movement in Social Work.*

7. Fisher, *Response of Social Work to the Depression,* 111. See also Chambers, *Paul U. Kellogg and the* Survey, 160.

8. Chambers, *Paul U. Kellogg and the* Survey, 160.

9. Ibid.

10. Jacob Fisher to Edith Abbott, December 22, 1936, Jacob Fisher Papers, National Coordinating Committee of Social Service Employees, 1935–37, box F534 (6), file 8, Charles Babbage Institute, Social Welfare History Archives, University of Minnesota, Minneapolis.

11. Edith Abbott to Jacob Fisher, December 11, 1936, Fisher Papers, box F534(6), file 8, Charles Babbage Institute, Social Welfare History Archives, University of Minnesota, Minneapolis.

12. Ibid.

13. Ibid.

14. *Trade Union Notes: National Conference of Social Work,* May 23, 1937, Fisher Papers, box F534 (6), file 9, Charles Babbage Institute, Social Welfare History Archives, University of Minnesota, Minneapolis.

15. Ehrenreich, *Altruistic Imagination,* chap. 4. See also Thyer and Biggerstaff, *Professional Social Work Credentialing and Legal Regulation,* 16; Barker, *Social Work Dictionary,* 189; *Proceedings of the National Conference of Social Work,* Sixty-Fourth Annual Session, 1937.

16. Grothaus, "Inevitable Mr. Gaines." See also Tushnet, *NAACP's Legal Strategy against Segregated Education,* 70–81; Sullivan, "Southern Reformers, the New Deal, and the Movement's Foundation," 84–85; Goldfield, *Black, White, and Southern,* 58.

17. Sawyer, "Gaines Case," 152–97. See also Kluger, *Simple Justice,* 202–4; Tushnet, *Making Civil Rights Law,* 70.

18. Sawyer, "Gaines Case," 21. See also Franklin, "American Values, Social Goals, and the Desegregated School," 200–201.

19. Sawyer, "Gaines Case," 23.

20. Hine, "Black Lawyers and the Twentieth-Century Struggle for Constitutional Change." See also Franklin and McNeil, *African Americans and the Living Constitution.*

21. Tushnet, *NAACP's Legal Strategy against Segregated Education,* chap. 5.

22. *Missouri ex rel. Gaines v. Canada* (305 U. S. 337), *Guide to the U. S. Supreme Court,* 903.

23. Tussman, *Supreme Court on Racial Discrimination,* 23.

24. Tushnet, *NAACP's Legal Strategy against Segregated Education,* 72.

25. Ibid., 74–75. See also McNeil, *Groundwork,* 142–51; and Bluford, "Lloyd Gaines Story."

26. Qtd. in Tushnet, *NAACP's Legal Strategy against Segregated Education,* 75.

27. Sullivan, "Southern Reformers, the New Deal, and the Movement's Foundation," 84.

28. Wesley, "Graduate Education for Negroes in Southern Universities," 91.

29. Kluger, *Simple Justice,* 157.

30. Ibid.

31. Thorpe, *Concise History of North Carolina Central University.* See also Armfield, "Durham's Tobacco Industry," 13–16.

32. Weare, "Charles Clinton Spaulding," 176.

33. Thorpe, *Concise History of North Carolina Central University,* 14.

34. James E. Shepard to Dr. Marion Hathway, Council on Social Work Education (CSWE), November 17, 1939, box 329, folder 2: North Carolina College for Negroes, Charles Babbage Institute, Social Welfare History Archives, University of Minnesota, Minneapolis.

35. Ibid.

36. Ibid.

37. Mr. Roy M. Brown to Marion Hathway, CSWE, December 22, 1939, box 329, folder 3: North Carolina College for Negroes, Charles Babbage Institute, Social Welfare History Archives, University of Minnesota, Minneapolis.

38. Marion Hathway, CSWE, to James E. Shepard, January 20, 1940, box 329, folder 12: North Carolina College for Negroes, Charles Babbage Institute, Social Welfare History Archives, University of Minnesota, Minneapolis.

39. James E. Shepard to Marion Hathway, CSWE, January 23, 1940, box 329, folder 12: North Carolina College for Negroes, Charles Babbage Institute, Social Welfare History Archives, University of Minnesota, Minneapolis.

40. Ibid.

41. James E. Shepard to Marion Hathway, CSWE, memorandum, January 23, 1940, box 329, folder 12: North Carolina College for Negroes, Charles Babbage Institute, Social Welfare History Archives, University of Minnesota, Minneapolis.

42. Ibid.

43. Ibid.

44. Ibid.

45. Roy Brown to Marion Hathway, CSWE, February 12, 1940, box 329, folder 12: North Carolina College for Negroes, Charles Babbage Institute, Social Welfare History Archives, University of Minnesota, Minneapolis.

46. Marion Hathway, CSWE, to James E. Shepard, February 20, 1940, box 329, folder 12: North Carolina College for Negroes, Charles Babbage Institute, Social Welfare History Archives, University of Minnesota, Minneapolis.

47. James E. Shepard to Marion Hathway, CSWE, March 1, 1940, box 329, folder 12: North Carolina College for Negroes, Charles Babbage Institute, Social Welfare History Archives, University of Minnesota, Minneapolis.

48. Thorpe, *Concise History of North Carolina Central University*, 14.

49. Myrdal, *American Dilemma*, 841.

50. Eugene Kinckle Jones to Charles S. Johnson, June 24, 1938, Charles S. Johnson Collection, box 26, folder 7, Amistad Research Center, Tulane University, New Orleans.

51. Sullivan, "Southern Reformers, the New Deal, and the Movement's Foundation," 84–85.

52. Ibid.

53. Claudia C. Andrews to Mrs. David Alter, April 8, 1939, NUL Papers, series IV, box 7, Julius Rosenwald Fund, 1930–33 and 1936–37, Library of Congress, Washington, D.C.

54. Ibid.

55. Ibid.

56. Parris and Brooks, *Blacks in the City*, 260–79.

57. Ibid., 260.

58. Ibid., 262.

59. Ibid., 263.

60. See ibid.

61. Ibid., 267.

62. Ibid.

63. Ibid., 271.

64. Ibid., 273.

65. Ibid.

66. Brown, "Social Work Leader in the Struggle for Racial Equality," 267.

67. Ibid., 266–80.

68. Parris and Brooks, *Blacks in the City,* 275.

69. Myrdal, *American Dilemma,* 837. See also *Abridged Autobiography of Eugene Kinckle Jones,* dictated to Gunnar Myrdal, 1940, NUL Papers, Collections of the Manuscript Division, Library of Congress, Washington, D.C. Jones is not quoted in Myrdal's work, but along with L. Hollingsworth Wood and Lester B. Granger of the NUL, he is given credit in footnotes for much of the information compiled concerning the Urban League. Myrdal made use of Jones's autobiography (see 837–38).

70. See Quarles, "A. Philip Randolph," 139–65. See also Karson and Radosh, "American Federation of Labor and the Negro Worker," 161–62.

71. Quarles, "A. Philip Randolph," 147.

72. Ibid. See also Pfeffer, *A. Philip Randolph*; and Harris, *Keeping the Faith.*

73. See Hine, *Path to Equality*; Kelley, *Hammer and Hoe.*

74. Author's interview with Betty Jones Dowling, June 15, 1995, Washington, D.C. Jones's granddaughter remembers her grandfather leaving for Arizona during the winter months; the family would have to await his return in March or April for important family decisions.

75. Application Form, "Terms of Affiliation," NUL Papers, series 5, box 4: Jones, General Secretary, Manuscript Division, Library of Congress, Washington, D.C.

76. Eugene Kinckle Jones to Charles S. Johnson, June 22, 1945, Charles S. Johnson Collection, box 12, file 12, Amistad Research Center, Tulane University, New Orleans.

77. Ibid.

78. "Discrimination Viewed in City," *Arizona Daily Star,* April 3, 1947, NUL Papers, series 5, box 4: Jones, General Secretary, Manuscript Division, Library of Congress, Washington, D.C.

79. Eugene Kinckle Jones, "Urban League Secretary Addresses Interracial Forum—Interracial Review News Service," NUL Papers, series 1, box 26: Jones Personal File—1948, Manuscript Division, Library of Congress, Washington, D.C.

80. Author's interview with Betty Jones Dowling. Dowling spoke of her grandfather's great fondness for his boyhood home; the family made an annual trip to Richmond and Virginia Union for homecoming. .

81. J. Harvey Kerns to Eugene Kinckle Jones, June 10, 1948, NUL Papers, series 1, box 26, Manuscript Division, Library of Congress, Washington, D.C.

82. Eugene Kinckle Jones to J. Harvey Kerns, memorandum, June 11, 1948, NUL Papers, series 1, box 26, Manuscript Division, Library of Congress, Washington, D.C.

83. John Malcus Ellison to Eugene Kinckle Jones, July 8, 1948, NUL Papers, series 1, box 26, Manuscript Division, Library of Congress, Washington, D.C.

84. Eugene Kinckle Jones to John M. Ellison, July 12, 1948, NUL Papers, series 1, box 26, Manuscript Division, Library of Congress, Washington, D.C.

85. Eugene Kinckle Jones, review of *The Negro Ghetto,* by Robert Weaver, *News,* NUL Papers, series 1, box 35, Manuscript Division, Library of Congress, Washington, D.C.

86. Ibid.

87. "Negro Rights Champion Recalls the Good Fight," *New York World-Telegram and Sun,* Thursday, May 17, 1951, NUL Papers, series 1, box 26, Manuscript Division, Library of Congress, Washington, D.C.

88. Ibid.

89. Author's interview with Betty Jones Dowling.

Conclusion

1. Thorpe, *Concise History of North Carolina Central University,* 73.

Bibliography

Primary Sources

Charles S. Johnson Papers, Amistad Research Center, Tulane University, New Orleans.
Eugene Kinckle Jones, Cornell University Alumni Files, Cornell University Library, Ithaca, New York.
Eugene Kinckle Jones Correspondence, Amistad Research Center, Tulane University, New Orleans.
Eugene Kinckle Jones Correspondence, National Urban League Papers, Library of Congress, Washington, D.C.
Eugene Kinckle Jones Correspondence, 1933–36, National Archives, Washington, D.C.
General Records of the Department of Commerce, National Archives, Washington, D.C.
Julius Rosenwald Papers, Amistad Research Center, Tulane University, New Orleans.
National Social Welfare History Archives, Council on Social Work Education, University of Minnesota, Minneapolis.
Records of the Bureau of Employment Security, National Archives, Washington, D.C.
Records of the Office of the Secretary of the Interior, National Archives, Washington, D.C.
Records of the Works Project Administration, National Archives, Washington, D.C.
Richmond and Lynchburg, Virginia, City Directories, 1880s–1890s, Virginia State Archives, Richmond.
W. E. B. DuBois Papers, microfilm, University of Massachusetts, Amherst.

Government Publications

Historical Statistics of the United States: Colonial Times to 1970, Bicentennial ed., Part 1, U.S. Department of Commerce Washington, D.C.: U.S. Government Printing Office, 1975.

Interviews

Betty Jones Dowling, granddaughter of Eugene Kinckle Jones, June 15, 1995, Washington, D.C.
Francis Kornegay, executive secretary of the Detroit Urban League (ret.), 1994, Detroit.

Eugene Kinckle Jones's Publications

"The Negro in Community Life." *Proceedings of the National Conference of Social Work.* San Francisco: NCSW, 1929. 388.

"Negro Migration in New York State." *Opportunity* Vol. 4, No. 37 (January 1926): 7–11.

"The Negro's Struggle for Health." *Proceedings of the National Conference of Social Work.* Washington, D.C.: NCSW, 1923. 68–72.

Review of *The Negro in Our History,* by Carter G. Woodson. *The Messenger* 5 (May 1923): 704–22.

Review of *The Negro Ghetto,* by Robert C. Weaver. *News* (Summer 1948). Original manuscript: NUL Papers, series 4, box 3, Manuscript Division, Library of Congress, Washington, D.C.

"Social Work among Negroes." *Annals of the American Academy of Political and Social Science* 140 (November 1928): 287–93.

"Social Work among Negroes." *The Messenger,* 1921.

"Some Fundamental Factors in Regard to the Health of the Negro." *Proceedings of the National Conference of Social Workers.* Memphis: NCSW, 1928. 176–78.

Eugene Kinckle Jones's Speeches

"Go to High School, Go to College." WMCA radio, May 16, 1926. UL Papers, series, 4, box 3, Manuscript Division, Library of Congress, Washington, D.C.

"Negro Migration in New York State." Delivered at the New York State Conference of Charities and Corrections, Hotel Roosevelt, New York, December 11, 1925. UL Papers, series 4, box 3, Manuscript Division, Library of Congress, Washington, D.C.

"The Negro's Opportunity Today." West Virginia Collegiate Institute, Commencement Address, June 1926. UL Papers, series 4, box 3, Manuscript Division, Library of Congress, Washington, D.C.

Secondary Sources

BOOKS

Abbott, Grace. *From Relief to Social Security: The Development of the New Public Welfare Services and Their Administration.* Chicago: University of Chicago Press, 1941.

Addams, Jane. *Twenty Years at Hull-House.* New York: Signet, 1960.

Adero, Malaika, ed. *Up South: Stories, Studies, and Letters of This Century's African-American Migrations.* New York: New Press, 1993.

Anderson, Eric, and Alfred Moss Jr., eds. *The Facts of Reconstruction: Essays in Honor of John Hope Franklin.* Baton Rouge: Louisiana State University Press, 1991.

Anderson, James D. *The Education of Blacks in the South, 1860–1935.* Chapel Hill: University of North Carolina Press, 1988.

Aptheker, Herbert, ed. *The Correspondence of W. E. B. DuBois.* Vols. 1 and 2. Amherst: University of Massachusetts Press, 1976.

Avery, Sheldon. *Up from Washington: William Pickens and the Negro Struggle for Equality, 1900–1954.* London: Associated University Presses, 1989.

Ayers, Edward L. *The Promise of the New South: Life after Reconstruction.* New York: Oxford University Press, 1992.

Baker, Robert L. *The Social Work Dictionary.* Silver Spring, Md.: National Association of Social Workers, 1987.

Bishop, Morris. *A History of Cornell.* Ithaca, N.Y.: Cornell University Press, 1962.

Biskupic, Joan, and Elder Witt, eds. *Congressional Quarterly's Guide to the U. S. Supreme Court.* 2d ed. Washington, D.C.: Congressional Quarterly, 1996.

Blackwell, James E., and Morris Janowitz, eds. *Black Sociologists: Historical and Contemporary Perspectives.* Chicago: University of Chicago Press, 1974.

Blum, John Morton. *The Progressive Presidents: Roosevelt, Wilson, Roosevelt, Johnson.* New York: W. W. Norton and Co., 1980.

Bracey, John H. Jr., August Meier, and Elliott Rudwick, eds. *Black Workers and Organized Labor.* Belmont, Calif.: Wadworth Publishing, 1971.

Brooks, John Graham. *An American Citizen: The Life of William Henry Baldwin Jr.* Boston: Houghton Mifflin, 1910.

Brown, Josephine Chapin. *Public Relief, 1929–1939.* New York: Octagon Books, 1971.

Cayton, Horace R., and George S. Mitchell. *Black Workers and the New Unions.* Westport, Conn.: Negro Universities Press, 1970.

Chambers, Clarke A., ed. *The New Deal at Home and Abroad, 1929–1945.* New York: Free Press, 1965.

——. *Paul U. Kellogg and the* Survey: *Voices for Social Welfare and Social Justice.* Minneapolis: University of Minnesota Press, 1971.

——. *Seedtime of Reform: American Social Service and Social Action, 1918–1933.* Minneapolis: University of Minnesota Press, 1963.

Chapin, F. Stuart, and Stuart A. Queen. *Research Memorandum on Social Work in the Depression.* New York: Arno Press, 1972.

Chesson, Michael. *Richmond after the War, 1865–1890.* Richmond: Virginia State Library, 1981.

Corey, Charles H. *A History of the Richmond Theological Seminary with Reminiscences of Thirty Years' Work among the Colored People of the South.* Richmond, Va.: J. W. Randolph, 1895.

Crocker, Ruth Hutchinson. *Social Work and Social Order: The Settlement Movement in Two Industrial Cities, 1889–1930.* Urbana: University of Illinois Press, 1992.

Dabney, Virginius. *Richmond: The Story of a City.* Garden City, N.Y.: Doubleday, 1976.

Dancy, John C. *Sand against the Wind: The Memoirs of John C. Dancy.* Detroit: Wayne State University Press, 1966.

Devine, Edward T. *When Social Work Was Young.* New York: MacMillan, 1939.

Ehrenreich, John H. *The Altruistic Imagination: A History of Social Work and Social Policy in the United States.* Ithaca, N.Y.: Cornell University Press, 1985.

Ellsworth, Scott. *Death in the Promised Land: The Tulsa Race Riot of 1921.* Baton Rouge: Louisiana State University Press, 1982.

Engs, Robert Francis. *Freedom's First Generation: Black Hampton, Virginia, 1861–1890.* Philadelphia: University of Pennsylvania Press, 1979.

Ferguson, Elizabeth A. *Social Work: An Introduction.* Philadelphia: J. B. Lippincott, 1963.

Fireside, Harvey. Plessy v. Ferguson: *Separate but Equal?* Springfield, N.J.: Enslow, 1997.

Fisher, Jacob. *The Response of Social Work to the Depression.* Boston: G. K. Hall and Co., 1980.

Foner, Philip S. *Organized Labor and the Black Worker, 1619–1973.* New York: Praeger, 1974.

Foner, Eric. *Reconstruction: America's Unfinished Revolution, 1863–1877.* New York: Harper and Row, 1988.

Frankel, Noralee, and Nancy S. Dye. *Gender, Class, Race, and Reform in the Progressive Era.* Lexington: University Press of Kentucky, 1991.

Franklin, John Hope, and August Meier, eds. *Black Leaders of the Twentieth Century.* Urbana: University of Illinois Press, 1982.

Franklin, John Hope, and Genna Rae McNeil, eds. *African Americans and the Living Constitution.* Washington, D.C.: Smithsonian Institution Press, 1995.

Franklin, Vincent P., and James D. Anderson, eds. *New Perspectives on Black Educational History.* Boston: G. K. Hall and Co., 1978.

Frazier, E. Franklin. *Black Bourgeoisie.* Glencoe, Ill.: Free Press, 1957.

———. *The Negro Family in the United States.* Chicago: University of Chicago Press, 1931.

———. *The Negro Race in Chicago.* Rev. ed. New York: Macmillan, 1957.

Gaines, Kevin K. *Uplifting the Race: Black Leadership, Politics, and Culture in the Twentieth Century.* Chapel Hill: University of North Carolina Press, 1996.

Gamble, Vanessa Northington. *Making a Place for Ourselves: The Black Hospital Movement, 1920–1945.* New York: Oxford University Press, 1995.

Gatewood, Willard B. *Aristocrats of Color: The Black Elite, 1880–1920.* Bloomington: Indiana University Press, 1990.

———. *Black Americans and the White Man's Burden, 1898–1903.* Urbana: University of Illinois Press, 1975.

Gavins, Raymond. *The Perils and Prospects of Southern Black Leadership: Gordon Blaine Hancock, 1884–1970.* Durham, N.C.: Duke University Press, 1977.

Giddings, Paula. *When and Where I Enter: The Impact of Black Women on Race and Sex in America.* New York: Bantam Books, 1984.

Goggin, Jacqueline. *Carter G. Woodson: A Life in Black History.* Baton Rouge: Louisiana State University Press, 1993.

Goldfield, David R. *Black, White, and Southern: Race Relations and Southern Culture, 1940 to the Present.* Baton Rouge: Louisiana State University Press, 1990.

Gottlieb, Peter. *Making Their Own Way: Southern Blacks' Migration to Pittsburgh, 1916–1930.* Urbana: University of Illinois Press, 1987.

Grant, Nancy L. *TVA and Black Americans: Planning for the Status Quo.* Philadelphia: Temple University Press, 1990.

Grant, Robert B. *The Black Man Comes to the City: A Documentary Account from the Great Migration to the Great Depression, 1915–1930.* Chicago: Nelson-Hall, 1972.

Green, Lorenzo J. *Selling Black History for Carter G. Woodson: A Diary, 1930–1933.* Ed. Arvarh E. Strickland. Columbia: University of Missouri Press, 1996.

Grossman, James R. *Land of Hope: Chicago, Black Southerners, and the Great Migration.* Chicago: University of Chicago Press, 1989.

Hammond, L. H. *In the Vanguard of a Race.* New York: Arno Press, 1972.

Handlin, Oscar. *The Newcomers: Negroes and Puerto Ricans in a Changing Metropolis.* Cambridge, Mass.: Harvard University Press, 1959.

Harding, Vincent. *There Is a River: The Black Struggle for Freedom in America.* New York: Harcourt Brace Javanovich, 1981.

Harlan, Louis R. *Booker T. Washington: The Making of a Black Leader, 1856–1901.* London: Oxford University Press, 1972.

———. *Booker T. Washington: The Wizard of Tuskegee, 1901–1915.* New York: Oxford University Press, 1983.

Harley, Sharon, and Rosalyn Terborg-Penn, eds. *The Afro-American Woman: Struggles and Images.* Port Washington, N.Y.: Kennikat Press, 1978.

Harris, William H. *The Harder We Run: Black Workers since the Civil War.* New York: Oxford University Press, 1982.

———. *Keeping the Faith: A Phillip Randolph, Milton P. Webster, and the Brotherhood of Sleeping Car Porters, 1925–37.* Urbana: University of Illinois Press, 1977.

Harrison, Alferdteen, ed. *Black Exodus: The Great Migration from the American South.* Jackson: University Press of Mississippi, 1991.

Henri, Florette. *Black Migration: Movement North, 1900–1920.* New York: Anchor/Doubleday, 1976.

Hewitt, Nancy A., and Suzanne Lebsock eds. *Visible Women: New Essays on American Activism.* Urbana: University of Illinois Press, 1993.

Hine, Darlene Clark. *Black Women in White: Racial Conflict and Cooperation in the Nursing Profession, 1890–1950.* Bloomington: Indiana University Press, 1989.

———. *Hine Sight: Black Women and the Re-Construction of American History.* Brooklyn: Carlson Publishing, 1994.

———. *The Path to Equality: From the Scottsboro Case to the Breaking of Baseball's Color Barrier (1931–1947).* New York: Chelsea House, 1995.

———. *Speak Truth to Power: Black Professional Class in United States History.* Brooklyn: Carlson Publishing, 1996.

Holt, Rackham. *Mary McLeod Bethune: A Biography.* Garden City, N.Y.: Doubleday, 1964.

Ickes, Harold L. *The Secret Diary of Harold L. Ickes: The First Thousand Days, 1933–1936.* New York: Simon and Schuster, 1953.

Jackson, Giles B., and D. Webster Davis. *The Industrial History of the Negro Race of the United States.* Freeport, N.Y.: Books for Libraries Press, 1971.

Jacobson, Julius, ed. *The Negro and the American Labor Movement.* Garden City, N.Y.: Doubleday, 1968.

Johnson, Charles S. *The Negro in Chicago: A Study of Race Relations and a Race Riot.* Chicago: University of Chicago Press, 1922.

Johnson, James Weldon. *Black Manhattan.* New York: Arno Press, 1930.

Jones, Adrienne Lash. *Jane Edna Hunter: A Case Study of Black Leadership, 1910–1950.* Brooklyn: Carlson Publishing, 1990.

Jones, Beverly Washington. *Quest for Equality: The Life and Writings of Mary Eliza Church Terrell, 1863–1954.* Brooklyn: Carlson Publishing, 1990.

Jones, Jacqueline. *Labor of Love, Labor of Sorrow: Black Women, Work, and the Family from Slavery to Present.* New York: Basic Books, 1985.

Katz, Michael B. *In the Shadow of the Poorhouse: A Social History of Welfare in America.* New York: Basic Books, 1986.

Katzman, David M. *Before the Ghetto: Black Detroit in the Nineteenth Century.* Urbana: University of Illinois Press, 1973.

Kelly, Robin D. G. *Hammer and Hoe: Alabama Communists during the Great Depression.* Chapel Hill: University of North Carolina Press, 1990.

Kirby, John B. *Black Americans in the Roosevelt Era: Liberalism and Race.* Knoxville: University of Tennessee Press, 1980.

Kluger, Richard. *Simple Justice: The History of* Brown v. Board of Education *and Black America's Struggle for Equality.* New York: Alfred A. Knopf, 1976.

Knupfer, Anne Meis. *Toward a Tenderer Humanity and a Nobler Womanhood: African American Women's Clubs in Turn-of-the-Century Chicago.* New York: New York University Press, 1996.

Kornweibel, Theodore Jr. *No Crystal Stair: Black Life and the* Messenger, *1917–1928.* Westport, Conn.: Greenwood Press, 1975.

Kusmer, Kenneth L. *A Ghetto Takes Shape: Black Cleveland, 1870–1930.* Urbana: University of Illinois Press, 1976.

Larson, Magali Sarfatti. *The Rise of Professionalism: A Sociological Analysis.* Berkeley: University of California Press, 1977.

Lasch-Quinn, Elisabeth. *Black Neighbors: Race and the Limits of Reform in the American Settlement House Movement, 1890–1945.* Chapel Hill: University of North Carolina Press, 1993.

Leiby, James. *A History of Social Welfare and Social Work in the United States.* New York: Columbia University Press, 1987.

Lewis, David Levering. *W. E. B. DuBois: Biography of a Race, 1868–1919.* New York: Henry Holt and Co., 1993.

———. *When Harlem Was in Vogue.* New York: Oxford University Press, 1981.

Lewis, Earl. *In Their Own Interests: Race, Class, and Power in Twentieth-Century Norfolk.* Berkeley: University of California Press, 1991.

Levy, Charles S. *Social Work Education, 1898–1955.* Washington, D.C.: National Association of Social Workers, 1981.

Litwack, Leon F. *Been in the Storm So Long: The Aftermath of Slavery.* New York: Alfred A. Knopf, 1979.

Locke, Alain, ed. *The New Negro: An Interpretation.* New York: Arno Press, 1968.

Logan, Rayford W. *Howard University: The First Hundred Years, 1867–1967.* New York: New York University Press, 1969.

———. *The Negro in American Life and Thought: The Nadir, 1877–1901.* New York: Dial Press, 1954.

Lubove, Roy. *The Struggle for Social Security, 1900–1935.* Cambridge, Mass.: Harvard University Press, 1968.

Luker, Ralph E. *The Social Gospel in Black and White: American Racial Reform, 1885–1912.* Chapel Hill: University of North Carolina Press, 1991.

Lynch, Hollis R. *The Black Urban Condition: A Documentary History, 1866–1971.* New York: Crowell, 1972.

Manning, Kenneth R. *Black Apollo of Science: The Life of Ernest Everett Just.* New York: Oxford University Press, 1983.

Marks, Carole. *Farewell—We're Good and Gone: The Great Black Migration*. Bloomington: Indiana University Press, 1989.

Martin, Elmer P., and Joanne Mitchell Martin. *Social Work and the Black Experience*. Washington, D.C.: National Association of Social Workers Press, 1995.

McMurry, Linda O. *George Washington Carver: Scientist and Symbol*. Oxford: Oxford University Press, 1981.

———. *Recorder of the Black Experience: A Biography of Monroe Nathan Work*. Baton Rouge: Louisiana State University Press, 1985.

McNeil, Genna Rae. *Groundwork: Charles Hamilton Houston and the Struggle for Civil Rights*. Philadelphia: University of Pennsylvania Press, 1983.

Meier, August. *Negro Thought in America, 1880–1915: Racial Ideologies in the Age of Booker T. Washington*. Ann Arbor: University of Michigan Press, 1963.

Meier, August, and Elliott Rudwick. *Black Detroit and the Rise of the UAW*. New York: Oxford University Press, 1979.

———. *Black History and the Historical Profession, 1915–1980*. Urbana: University of Illinois Press, 1986.

———. *From Plantation to Ghetto: An Interpretive History of American Negroes*. New York: Hill and Wang, 1966.

Meier, August, Elliott Rudwick, and Francis L. Broderick. *Black Protest Thought in the Twentieth Century*. 2nd ed. Indianapolis: Bobbs-Merrill, 1965.

Meier, Elizabeth G. *A History of the New York School of Social Work*. New York: Columbia University Press, 1954.

Meyer, Carol H. *Social Work Practice: A Response to the Urban Crisis*. New York: Free Press, 1976.

Miller, Randall M., and Paul A. Cimbala, eds. *American Reform and Reformers: A Biographical Dictionary*. Westport, Conn.: Greenwood Press, 1996.

Mitchell, Michele. *Righteous Propagation: African Americans and the Politics of Racial Destiny after Reconstruction*. Chapel Hill: University of North Carolina Press. 2004.

Moore, Jesse Thomas Jr. *A Search for Equality: The National Urban League, 1910–1961*. University Park: Pennsylvania State University Press, 1981.

Morton, Richard L. *The Negro in Virginia Politics, 1865–1902*. Spartanburg, S.C.: Reprint Co., 1973.

Moss, Alfred A. Jr. *The American Negro Academy: Voice of the Talented Tenth*. Baton Rouge: Louisiana State University Press, 1981.

Myrdal, Gunnar. *An American Dilemma*. New York: Harper and Row, 1944.

Natanson, Nicholas. *The Black Image in the New Deal: The Politics of FSA Photography*. Knoxville: University of Tennessee Press, 1992.

Neverdon-Morton, Cynthia. *Afro-American Women of the South and the Advancement of the Race, 1895–1925*. Knoxville: University of Tennessee Press, 1989.

Novak, Daniel A. *The Wheel of Servitude: Black Forced Labor after Slavery*. Lexington: University of Press of Kentucky, 1978.

Ovington, Mary White. *Portraits in Color*. New York: Viking Press, 1927.

Painter, Nell Irvin. *Exodusters: Black Migration to Kansas after Reconstruction*. Lawrence: University of Kansas Press, 1986.

——. *Standing at Armageddon: The United States, 1877–1919.* New York: W. W. Norton, 1987.

Parris, Guichard, and Lester Brooks. *Blacks in the City: A History of the National Urban League.* Boston: Little, Brown, 1971.

Pfeffer, Paula F. *A. Philip Randolph, Pioneer of the Civil Rights Movement.* Baton Rouge: Louisiana State University Press, 1990.

Pickens, William. *Bursting Bonds: The Autobiography of a "New Negro."* Edited by William L. Andrews. Notre Dame: University of Notre Dame Press, 2002.

Platt, Anthony M. *E. Franklin Frazier Reconsidered.* New Brunswick, N.J.: Rutgers University Press, 1991.

Rabinowitz, Howard N. *Race Relations in the Urban South, 1865–1890.* New York: Oxford University Press, 1978.

——, ed. *Southern Black Leaders of the Reconstruction Era.* Urbana: University of Illinois Press, 1982.

Rachleff, Peter. *Black Labor in Richmond, 1865–1890.* Urbana: University of Illinois Press, 1989.

Reed, Christopher Robert. *"All the World Is Here!": The Black Presence at White City.* Bloomington: Indiana University Press, 2000.

——. *The Chicago NAACP and the Rise of Black Professional Leadership, 1910–1966.* Bloomington: Indiana University Press, 1997.

Reisch, Michael, and Janice Andrews. *The Road Not Taken: A History of Radical Social Work in the United States.* New York: Brunner-Routledge, 2002.

Richardson, Joe M. *Christian Reconstruction: The American Missionary Association and Southern Blacks, 1861–1890.* Athens: University of Georgia Press, 1986.

——. *A History of Fisk University, 1865–1946.* Tuscaloosa: University of Alabama Press, 1980.

Robinson, Armstead L., and Patricia Sullivan, eds. *New Directions in Civil Rights Studies.* Charlottesville: University Press of Virginia, 1991.

Ross, Edyth L., ed. *Black Heritage in Social Welfare, 1860–1930.* Metuchen, N.J.: Scarecrow Press, 1978.

Rouse, Jacqueline Anne. *Lugenia Burns Hope: Black Southern Reformer.* Athens: University of Georgia Press, 1989.

Rudwick, Elliott M. *Race Riot at East St. Louis, July 2, 1917.* Carbondale: Southern Illinois University Press, 1964.

Salmond, John A. *A Southern Rebel: The Life and Times of Aubrey Willis Williams, 1890–1965.* Chapel Hill: University of North Carolina Press, 1983.

Santino, Jack. *Miles of Smiles, Years of Struggle: Stories of Black Pullman Porters.* Urbana: University of Illinois Press, 1989.

Scott, James C. *Domination and the Arts of Resistance: Hidden Transcripts.* New Haven, Conn.: Yale University Press, 1990.

Scruggs, L. A. *Women of Distinction: Remarkable in Works and Invincible in Character.* Raleigh, N.C.: N.p., 1892.

Senechal, Roberta. *The Sociogenesis of a Race Riot: Springfield, Illinois, in 1908.* Urbana: University of Illinois Press, 1990.

Sherman, Richard, ed. *The Negro and the City.* New York: Prentice-Hall, 1970.

Shaw, Stephanie J. *What a Woman Ought to Be and to Do: Black Professional Women Workers during the Jim Crow Era*. Chicago: University of Chicago Press, 1996.

Simmons, Rev. William J. *Men of Mark: Eminent, Progressive, and Rising*. New York: Arno Press, 1968.

Simon, Barbara Levy. *The Empowerment Tradition in American Social Work: A History*. New York: Columbia University Press, 1994.

Sinnette, Elinor Des Verney. *Arthur Alfonso Schomburg, Black Bibliophile and Collector: A Biography*. Detroit: Wayne State University Press, 1989.

Sitkoff, Harvard. *A New Deal for Blacks: The Emergence of Civil Rights as a National Issue*. Vol. 1, *The Depression Decade*. New York: Oxford University Press, 1978.

———. *The Struggle for Black Equality, 1954–1992*. Rev. ed. New York: Hill and Wang, 1993.

Spano, Rick. *The Rank and File Movement in Social Work*. Washington, D.C.: University Press of America, 1982.

Spero, Sterling D., and Abram L. Harris. *The Black Worker: The Negro Labor Movement*. New York: Atheneum, 1968.

Strickland, Arvarh E. *History of the Chicago Urban League*. Urbana: University of Illinois Press, 1966.

Summerville, James. *Educating Black Doctors: A History of Meharry Medical College*. Tuscaloosa: University of Alabama Press, 1983.

Taeuber, Karl, and Alma F. Taeuber. *Negroes in Cities: Residential Segregation and Neighborhood Change*. Chicago: Aldine Publishing Co., 1965.

Taylor, Alrutheus Ambush. *The Negro in the Reconstruction of Virginia*. Washington, D.C.: Association for the Study of Negro Life and History, 1926.

Terrell, Mary Church. *A Colored Woman in a White World*. Washington, D.C.: Randall, 1940.

Thomas, Richard W. *Life for Us Is What We Make It: Building Black Community in Detroit, 1915–1945*. Bloomington: Indiana University Press, 1992.

Thoms, Adah B. *Pathfinders: A History of the Progress of Colored Graduate Nurses*. New York: Kay Printing House, 1929.

Thorpe, Earl E. *A Concise History of North Carolina Central University*. Durham, N.C.: Harrington Publications, 1984.

Thyer, Bruce A., and Marilyn A. Biggerstaff. *Professional Social Work Credentialing and Legal Regulation: A Review of Critical Issues and an Annotated Bibliography*. Springfield, Ill.: Charles C. Thomas, 1989.

Trolander, Judith Ann. *Professionalism and Social Change: From the Settlement House Movement to Neighborhood Centers, 1886 to the Present*. New York: Columbia University Press, 1987.

———. *Settlement Houses and the Great Depression*. Detroit: Wayne State University, 1975.

Trotter, Joe William Jr. *Black Milwaukee: The Making of an Industrial Proletariat, 1915–45*. Urbana: University of Illinois Press, 1985.

———, ed. *The Great Migration in Historical Perspective: New Dimensions of Race, Class, and Gender*. Bloomington: Indiana University Press, 1991.

Tushnet, Mark V. *Making Civil Rights Law: Thurgood Marshall and the Supreme Court, 1936–1961*. New York: Oxford University Press, 1994.

———. *The NAACP's Legal Strategy against Segregated Education, 1925–1950*. Chapel Hill: University of North Carolina Press, 1987.

Tussman, Joseph, ed. *The Supreme Court on Racial Discrimination.* New York: Oxford University Press, 1963.

Tuttle, William A. Jr. *Race Riot: Chicago in the Red Summer of 1919.* New York: Atheneum, 1970.

Vose, Clement E. *Caucasians Only: The Supreme Court, the NAACP, and the Restrictive Covenant Cases.* Berkeley: University of California Press, 1959.

Walker, Sydnor H. *Social Work and the Training of Social Workers.* Chapel Hill: University of North Carolina Press, 1928.

Wallace, Phyllis A. *Black Women in the Labor Force.* Cambridge: Massachusetts Institute of Technology Press, 1980.

Walton, Hanes Jr. *Black Republicans: The Politics of the Black and Tans.* Metuchen, N.J.: Scarecrow Press, 1975.

Walton, Ronald G. *Women in Social Work.* London: Routledge and Kegan Paul, 1975.

Ware, Susan. *Beyond Suffrage: Women in the New Deal.* Cambridge, Mass.: Harvard University Press, 1981.

———. *Holding Their Own: American Women in the 1930s.* Boston: Twayne, 1982.

Weaver, Robert C. *The Negro Ghetto.* New York: Harcourt, Brace, and Co., 1948.

———. *Negro Labor: A National Problem.* New York: Harcourt, Brace, and Co., 1946.

Weems, Robert E. Jr. *Desegregating the Dollar: African American Consumerism in the Twentieth Century.* New York: New York University Press, 1998.

Weiss, Nancy J. *Farewell to the Party of Lincoln: Black Politics in the Age of FDR.* Princeton, N.J.: Princeton University Press, 1983.

———. *The National Urban League, 1910–1940.* New York: Oxford University Press, 1974.

Wesley, Charles H. *Henry Arthur Callis: Life and Legacy.* Chicago: Foundation Publishers, 1977.

———. *The History of Alpha Phi Alpha: A Development in College Life.* Chicago: Foundation Publishers, 1929.

———. *Negro Labor in the United States, 1850–1925: A Study in American Economic History.* New York: Russell and Russell, 1967.

Williams, Lillian Serece. *Strangers in the Land of Paradise: The Creation of an African American Community, Buffalo, New York, 1900–1940.* Bloomington: Indiana University Press, 1999.

Wilson, Francille Rusan. *The Segregated Scholars: Black Social Scientists and the Creation of Black Labor Studies, 1890–1950.* Charlottesville: University Press of Virginia, 2006.

Wintz, Cary D., ed. *African American Political Thought, 1890–1930: Washington, DuBois, Garvey, and Randolph.* New York: M. E. Sharpe, 1996.

———. *Black Culture and the Harlem Renaissance.* Houston: Rice University Press, 1988.

Wolkinson, Benjamin W. *Blacks, Unions, and the EEOC: A Study of Administrative Futility.* Lexington, Mass.: D.C. Heath, 1973.

Woodroofe, Kathleen. *From Charity to Social Work in England and the United States.* Toronto: University of Toronto Press, 1962.

Woodson, Carter G. *A Century of Negro Migration.* Washington, D.C.: Association for the Study of Negro Life and History, 1918.

———. *The Negro in Our History.* Washington, D.C.: Associated Publishers, 1922.

Woodward, C. Vann. *The Strange Career of Jim Crow.* Rev. ed. New York: Oxford University Press, 1965.

Works Project Administration of Virginia. *The Negro in Virginia*. New York: Hastings House, 1940.

Wynes, Charles E. *Race Relations in Virginia, 1870–1902*. Totowa, N.J.: Rowman and Littlefield, 1971.

ESSAYS

Anderson, James D. "The Hampton Model of Normal School Industrial Education, 1868–1900." In *New Perspectives on Black Educational History*. Ed. James D. Anderson and Vincent P. Franklin. Boston: G. K. Hall, 1978. 61–96.

Brown, Annie Woodley, "A Social Work Leader in the Struggle for Racial Equality: Lester Blackwell Granger." *Social Service Review* 65.2 (June 1991): 266–80.

Brown, Elsa Barkley. "Womanish Consciousness: Maggie Lena Walker and the Independent Order of Saint Luke." *Signs* 14.3 (Spring 1989): 610–33.

Bluford, Lucile H. "The Lloyd Gaines Story." *Journal of Educational Sociology* 22.6 (February 1959): 242–46.

Carlton-LaNey, Iris. "The Career of Birdye Henrietta Haynes, a Pioneer Settlement Worker." *Social Service Review* 68 (June 1994): 254–73.

———. "Elizabeth Ross Haynes: An African American Reformer of Womanish Consciousness, 1908–1940." *Social Work* 42.6 (August 1997): 573–84.

———. "Training African-American Social Workers through the NUL Fellowship Program." *Journal of Sociology and Social Welfare* 21.1 (March 1994): 43–54.

Chafe, William H. "Women's History and Political History: Some Thoughts on Progressivism and the New Deal." In *Visible Women: New Essays on American Activism*. Ed. Nancy A. Hewitt and Suzanne Lebsock. Urbana: University of Illinois Press, 1993. 101–18.

Chambers, Clarke A. "Women in the Creation of the Profession of Social Work." *Social Service Review* 60 (1986): 1–33.

Chesson, Michael B. "Richmond's Black Councilmen, 1871–96." In *Southern Black Leaders of the Reconstruction Era*. Ed. Howard N. Rabinowitz. Urbana: University of Illinois Press, 1982. 191–222.

Cohn, William. "The Great Migration as a Lever for Social Change." In *Black Exodus: The Great Migration from the American South*. Ed. Alferdteen Harrison. Jackson: University Press of Mississippi, 1991. 73–78.

Cromwell, Cheryl D. "Black Women as Pioneers in Social Welfare." *Journal of Sociology and Social Welfare* 1 (March 1994).

Fogel, David. "Social Work and Negroes." *Phylon* 18 (1957): 277–85.

Franklin, Vincent P. "American Values, Social Goals, and the Desegregated School: A Historical Perspective." In *New Perspectives on Black Educational History*. Ed. Vincent P. Franklin and James D. Anderson. Boston: G. K. Hall and Co., 1978. 193–211.

Gary, Rogenia Baker, and Lawrence E. Gary. "The History of Social Work Education for Black People, 1900–1930." *Journal of Sociology and Social Welfare* 21.1 (March 1994): 67–82.

Gershenhorn, Jerry. "*Hocutt v. Wilson* and Race Relations in Durham, North Carolina, during the 1930s." *North Carolina Historical Review* 78.3 (July 2001): 275–308.

Gottlieb, Peter. "Rethinking the Great Migration: A Perspective from Pittsburgh." In *The Great Migration in Historical Perspective: New Dimensions of Race, Class, and Gender*. Ed. Joe William Trotter Jr. Bloomington: Indiana University Press, 1991. 68–82.

———. "The White Man's Union: The Great Migration and the Resonance of Race and

Class in Chicago, 1916–1922." In *The Great Migration in Historical Perspective: New Di-mensions of Race, Class, and Gender*. Ed. Joe William Trotter Jr. Bloomington: Indiana University Press, 1991. 83–105.

Grothaus, Larry. "The Inevitable Mr. Gaines: The Long Struggle to Desegregate the Uni-versity of Missouri, 1936–1950." *Arizona and the West* 26.1 (Spring 1984): 20–42.

Harley, Sharon. "Mary Church Terrell, Genteel Militant." In *Black Leaders of the Nine-teenth Century*. Ed. Leon Litwack and August Meier. Urbana: University of Illinois Press, 1988. 307–21.

Hill, T. Arnold, "Labor: Open Letter to Mr. William Green, American Federation of Labor." *Opportunity* 8 (February 1930): 56–57.

Hill, Walter B. Jr. "Finding a Place for the Negro: Robert C. Weaver and the Groundwork for the Civil Rights Movement." *Prologue* 37.1 (Spring 2005): 42–51.

Hine, Darlene Clark. "Black Lawyers and the Twentieth-Century Struggle for Consti-tutional Change." In *Speak Truth to Power: Black Professional Class in United States History*. Brooklyn: Carlson Publishing, 1996. 147–68.

———. "Black Migration to the Urban Midwest: The Gender Dimension, 1915–1945." In *The Great Migration in Historical Perspective: New Dimensions of Race, Class, and Gen-der*. Ed. Joe William Trotter Jr. Bloomington: Indiana University Press, 1991. 127–46.

———. "Carter G. Woodson: White Philanthropy and Negro Historiography." In *Hine-Sight: Black Women and the Re-Construction of American History*. Brooklyn: Carlson, 1994. 203–22.

———. "The Housewives' League of Detroit: Black Women and Economic Nationalism." In *Hine Sight: Black Women and the Re-Construction of American History*. Brooklyn: Carlson Publishing, 1994. 129–46.

———. "'They Shall Mount Up with Wings as Eagles': Historical Images of Black Nurses, 1890–1950." In *HineSight: Black Women and the Re-Construction of American History*. Brooklyn: Carlson, 1994. 163–201.

Ives, Patricia Carter, "Giles Beecher Jackson: Jamestown Tercentennial of 1907." *Negro History Bulletin* 38.8 (December 1975): 480–83.

Johnson, Audreye E. "The Sin of Omission: African-American Women in Social Work." *Journal of Multicultural Social Work* 1.2 (1991): 1–15.

Jones, Butler E. "The Tradition of Sociology Teaching in Black Colleges: The Unheralded Professionals." In *Black Sociologists: Historical and Contemporary Perspectives*. Ed. James E. Blackwell and Morris Janowitz. Chicago: University of Chicago Press, 1974. 121–63.

Karson, Marc, and Ronald Radosh. "The American Federation of Labor and the Negro Worker, 1894–1949." In *The Negro and the American Labor Movement*. Ed. Julius Ja-cobson. New York: Doubleday, 1968. 158–87.

Knight, Louise W. "Jane Addams and the Settlement House Movement." In *American Reform and Reformers: A Biographical Dictionary*. Ed. Randall M. Miller and Paul A. Cimbala. Westport, Conn.: Greenwood Press, 1996. 85–98.

Kogut, Alvin B. "The Negro and the Charity Organization Society in the Progressive Era." In *Proceedings of the National Conference of Social Work*. Pittsburgh: NCSW, 1917.

Marks, Carole. "The Social and Economic Life of Southern Blacks during the Migration." In *Black Exodus: The Great Migration from the American South*. Ed. Alferdteen Har-rison. Jackson: University Press of Mississippi, 1991. 36–50.

Moneyhon, Carl H. "The Failure of Southern Republicanism, 1867–1876." In *The Facts of Reconstruction: Essays in Honor of John Hope Franklin*. Ed. Eric Anderson and Alfred Moss Jr. Baton Rouge: Louisiana State University Press, 1991. 99–119.

Popple, Philip R. "The Social Work Profession: A Reconceptualization." *Social Service Review* 59 (December 1985): 560–77.

Quarles, Benjamin. "A. Philip Randolph: Labor Leader at Large." In *Black Leaders of the Twentieth Century*. Ed. John Hope Franklin and August Meier. Urbana: University of Illinois Press, 1982. 138–65.

Robbins, Richard. "Charles S. Johnson." In *Black Sociologists: Historical and Contemporary Perspectives*. Ed. James E. Blackwell and Morris Janowitz. Chicago: University of Chicago Press, 1974. 56–84.

Ross, B. Joyce. "Mary McLeod Bethune and the National Youth Administration: A Case Study of Power Relationships in the Black Cabinet of Franklin D. Roosevelt." In *Black Leaders of the Twentieth Century*. Ed. John Hope Franklin and August Meier. Urbana: University of Illinois Press, 1982. 191–219.

Rudwick, Elliott. "W. E. B. DuBois as Sociologist." In *Black Sociologists: Historical and Contemporary Perspectives*. Ed. James E. Blackwell and Morris Janowitz. Chicago: University of Chicago Press, 1974. 25–55.

Smith, Stanley H. "Sociological Research and Fisk University: A Case Study." In *Black Sociologists: Historical and Contemporary Perspectives*. Ed. James E. Blackwell and Morris Janowitz. Chicago: University of Chicago Press, 1974. 164–90.

Sullivan, Patricia. "Southern Reformers, the New Deal, and the Movement's Foundation." In *New Directions in Civil Rights Studies*. Ed. Armstead L. Robinson and Patricia Sullivan. Charlottesville: University Press of Virginia, 1991. 81–104.

Walkowitz, Daniel J. "The Making of a Feminine Professional Identity: Social Workers in the 1920s." *American Historical Review* 95.4 (October 1990): 1051–75.

Weare, Walter. "Charles Clinton Spaulding: Middle-Class Leadership in the Age of Segregation." In *Black Leaders of the Twentieth Century*. Ed. John Hope Franklin and August Meier. Urbana: University of Illinois Press, 1982. 167–89.

Weaver, Bill, and Oscar C. Page. "The Black Press and the Drive for Integrated Graduate and Professional Schools." *Phylon* 43 (1982): 15–28.

Wesley, Charles H. "Graduate Education for Negroes in Southern Universities." *Harvard Educational Review* 10 (1940): 82–94.

Williams, Fannie Barrier. "Social Bonds in the 'Black Belt' of Chicago: Negro Organizations and the New Spirit Pervading Them." *Charities* 15.1 (1905): 40–44.

Wye, Christopher G. "The New Deal and the Negro Community: Toward a Broader Conceptualization." *Journal of American History* 59 (December 1972): 621–39.

DISSERTATIONS AND THESES

Armfield, Felix L. "Durham's Tobacco Industry: The Black Experience, 1890–1950." Master's thesis, North Carolina Central University, 1989.

Brown, Elsa Barkley. "Uncle Ned's Children: Negotiating Community and Freedom in Postemancipation Richmond, Virginia." Ph.D. dissertation, Kent State University, 1994.

Hamilton, Dona Cooper. "The National Urban League during the Depression, 1930–1939: The Quest for Jobs for Black Workers." Ph.D. dissertation, Columbia University, 1982.

Hendricks, Wanda Ann. "The Politics of Race: Black Women in Illinois, 1890–1920." Ph.D. dissertation, Purdue University, 1990.

MacLeish, Marlene Y. Smith. "Medical Education in Black Colleges and Universities in the United States of America: An Analysis of the Emergence of Black Medical Schools Between 1867 and 1976." Ed.D. dissertation, Harvard University, 1978.

Perlman, Daniel. "Stirring the White Conscience: The Life of George Edumund Haynes." Ph.D. dissertation, New York University, 1972.

Sawyer, Robert McLaran. "The Gaines Case: Its Background and Influence on the University of Missouri and Lincoln University, 1936–1950." Ph.D. dissertation, University of Missouri, 1966.

Welch, Eloise Turner. "The Background and Development of the American Missionary Association's Decision to Educate Freedmen in the South, with Subsequent Repercussions." Ph.D. dissertation, Bryn Mawr College, 1976.

Index

FELIX L. ARMFIELD is a professor
of history at Buffalo State College
and the author of *Black Life in West
Central Illinois.*

The University of Illinois Press
is a founding member of the
Association of American University Presses.

Composed in 10.5/13 Adobe Minion Pro
with Univers Std Condensed display
at the University of Illinois Press
Manufactured by Sheridan Books, Inc.

University of Illinois Press
1325 South Oak Street
Champaign, IL 61820-6903
www.press.uillinois.edu